T0121508

WRITING

Mystery & Mayhem

WRITING

Mystery & Mayhem

Edited by

Irene Staunton

Published by Weaver Press, Box A1922, Avondale, Harare. 2015

<www.weaverpresszimbabwe.com>

© Each individual story, the author.
© This collection, Weaver Press, 2015.

Photographs of the authors: Godess Bvukutwa, Lawrence Hoba, Farai Mudzingwa, Naishe Nyamubaya, Jo Saunders, Valerie Tagwira (Weaver Press)
Sam Brakarsh (Barbara Kaim), Donna Kirstein (B. Blanchard/Hex-in Photography), Bongani Sibanda (Nicholas Sibindi), Chris Wilson (Humam Khan)

Cover Design: Danes Design, Harare.
Printed by: Directory Publishers, Bulawayo.

All rights reserved. No part of the publication may be reproduced, stored in a retrieval system or transmitted in any form by any means – electronic, mechanical, photocopying, recording, or otherwise – without the express written permission of the publisher.

ISBN: 978-1-77922-278-7

Contents

Authors' biographies

Jonathan Brakarsh is a writer and health professional. Writing helps him to unravel the confusion and contradictions of living in this world. He has been previously published by Weaver Press in the anthology, *Writing Free* and was a finalist in the 2012 *Opium* Magazine Short Story Competition. He is also the author of *The Journey of Life* and *Say and Play* which uses stories and games to engage young children in Africa to find solutions to life's challenges.

Sam Brakarsh was born in Hatfield, Harare in 1998. 'Bob liked Pinstripes' is his first published story. He is a keen actor and has recently performed in *Master Harold and the Boys* at the Harare International Festival of the Arts.

Godess Bvukutwa is a 28-year-old writer of both fiction and non-fiction. In 2012, she won the Zimbabwe Women Writers' Norma Kitson Short Story Award for 'Confessions Beyond the Tombstone'. Some of her non-fiction has been published on internet sites such as the International Museum of Women and This is Africa. An essay, 'Raise me to be a leader as well' appears in 'Hysteria', a radical feminist publication. Aside from writing, Godess is a women's rights activist and the founder of Mambakwedza Women's Centre, an organisation which works with under-privileged and under-served women and girls in Mashonaland West. Godess studied English and has an MA in Development Studies. She is married and has a baby girl.

Lawrence Hoba, born in 1983 in Masvingo, Zimbabwe is an author, blogger, entrepreneur and literature promoter. His collection of short stories, *The Trek and Other Stories* (2009) was nominated for the NAMA, 2010 and went on to win the ZBPA awards for Best Literature in English category. Hoba's short stories and poetry have also appeared in various anthologies. He maintains an active social media presence with key focus on the arts, politics and business.

Donna Kirstein grew up in Zimbabwe, where she developed a passion for sunshine and blue skies, reading and storytelling. Donna moved to England to study and now stands on the beach watching the waves rolling over the shingle. She has been published in *Writing Free*: an anthology of Zimbabwean writing.

Isabella Matambanadzo is a Zimbabwean feminist activist. She was taught to read and write by her maternal grandmother who, until her death, was a primary school teacher in rural villages in Zimbabwe. Isabella's writing is influenced by the various experiences that women have of life and living across the world. And by the stories women tell.

Farai Mudzingwa is a writer based in Harare. He dabbles in sports photography, sports conditioning and fitness training. He also contributes in the satirical publication *Mos Native Speaks*.

Naishe Hassan Nyamubaya is a student and public speaker, who was born in 1996 in Harare. Growing up on his mother's game farm, he did his primary education at Lendy Park School, before completing his secondary education at Watershed College. He has produced numerous creative works including award-winning speeches, and short stories. When not at work, he enjoys swimming and watching television.'Tsikamutanda' is his first published work. Currently he is a student looking to undertake film making and script writing at university.

Jo Saunders is 64 and lives with her husband, dog and Manx cat in a treed Harare home. She reads prolifically, especially fantasy fiction and mystery, and has been writing all her life but only started finishing stories a few years ago. She enjoys listening to stories told by their workers about the lives of their extended families, and occasionally visits their *kumusha* villages.

Bongani Sibanda was born in Matabeleland South, Zimbabwe, at Mfila Village. Attended Zwehamba and Nyashongwe primary schools. He attended Shashane and Tshelanyemba schools for his secondary education, graduating from the latter in 2008. Based in Johannesburg, South Africa, he has finished a collection of short stories, and currently working on his first novel.

Valerie Tagwira is a specialist obstetrician and gynaecologist. She practices in Harare. *The Uncertainty of Hope*, her first novel, won the National Arts Merit Award (NAMA) for Outstanding Fiction Book in 2008. Her short story 'The Journey' was published in the Caine Prize Anthology 2010, and 'Mainini Grace's Promise' was published in *Women Writing Zimbabwe*. It was translated into Shona for the anthology *Mazambuko*.

Christopher Wilson was born in Gweru, grew up on a farm at Nyazura and went to school in Mutare, and studied literature at the University of

Cape Town. He has spent much of his adult life abroad, mainly in Egypt, Turkey, Yemen, Mozambique and currently Bahrain. He otherwise lives in Chimanimani. Chris was published in *Writing Still* (2003) and *Writing Now* (2005). His short story 'Whatever would Auntie Jean say?' was translated into Shona for the the anthology *Mazambuko*.

The General's Gun

Jonathan Brakarsh

In downtown Gweru, there's an auto dealership, Dynamo Motors. It specialises in Mercedes. It is the place to go in Gweru if one wants a Merc.

One day, a normal day, with traffic moving at a leisurely pace down Main Street, a kombi pulls up with its engine running. It has the message, '*God Knows*' written across the top of the windscreen in silver lettering. The driver is stone faced – either angry or scared. It's hard to tell. He has a smooth face, a woman's complexion. There's a great deal of noise inside the kombi – chanting and loud voices. The door slides open and out leaps a mass of writhing energy. The Youth Brigade. People outside this country have often asked how one makes a youth brigade. The recipe is as follows:

Take one unemployed, poorly educated youth
Throw in generous amounts of chibuku or mbanje
Add some cash

… and you have what just jumped out of the kombi. Seventeen of them to be exact. They're singing revolutionary songs and waving pangas; then they all rush into Dynamo Motors, attracted like dogs to a steak supper, touching all the beautiful new cars – silver ones, gold ones, blue ones and black ones.

The big-bellied Manager, sitting behind his expensive looking desk, looks up at seventeen red-eyed, panga-waving, ragged-looking youth with nothing to lose. He turns pale and feels his aging process accelerating. The leader of the group, with a white toothpaste smile, high cheekbones and the smooth stroke of a master batsman, sweeps his panga through the air and embeds it in the manager's desk, which shudders in response. 'Next time *ndinonyatso kunanga zvakanaka!* My aim is good,' he said. 'Next time, it's you!'

The youth with him are toy-toying, singing, eyes blazing under the fluorescent lighting of the Mercedes dealership. On the walls are large posters of beautiful women posing on shimmering Benzes. With great excitement, the youth jump down into the showroom area. They love the cars. They open the passenger doors and sit behind the wheels, laughing gleefully. The youth leader pronounces, 'By order of the Governor, this *bhizimisi* is now ours. We want *mari* and your cars. Now!'

The Manager feels a large space opening up in the pit of his stomach. 'I have to make a call,' he croaks, his throat dry and tight. The youth leader raises his panga again and axes it into the wood of the manager's desk, leaving a second noticeable gouge on the beautifully waxed surface. The Manager calls a number, and waits, while the perspiring islands of wetness on his shirt slowly merge together. He talks quietly into the phone, taking rapid breaths, speaking in jagged sentences. You can hear the tension in his voice, and the hope. The man on the other end of the line, says, 'Keep them busy for thirty minutes and I'll be there.' The Manager hangs up.

'Well Gentleman!' he says to the crowd milling disconsolately around his desk. Some are already looking through his drawers, some are playing with trophies they have found – a letter opener in the shape of a Mercedes, a cigarette lighter resembling a girl in a bikini – and some are waiting as if frozen in time.

'Well Gentlemen,' he says again, rising from his chair, always the salesman, always ready to sell to an interested customer, 'Can I show you around?' The group follows behind him, one of the youth intermittently giving him a hard push. He recovers his gait each time, pointing out this car and the next, proclaiming the wonders of owning a Mercedes. He enquires about the cars they presently drive. There is a silence, perhaps the hint of embarrassment and then anger. 'Shut the fuck up, white man,' one of the youth yells, hitting the Manager between the shoulder blades with the handle of his panga. The Manager's body crumples momentarily but he pulls himself up, regaining his composure. 'Gentlemen,' he says, 'would you like to see our newest model?'

The morning is passing. One of the youth orders, 'Make us tea and don't forget the *mukaka*, sugar and *chingwa*!' The Manager hears this command. You can see him calculating, knowing he'll never have enough bread to satisfy the hunger of the group. He calls to the tea-boy, 'Be kind enough to make tea for everyone here, please'. There is an exchange of glances between them and the message is clear.

'I will have to go next door to heat the water as our kettle is broken,' the tea-boy says. The tea-boy, a man with neatly groomed hair, a grey moustache, and black shoes brilliantly shined, walks at an unhurried pace to the kitchen.

The Manager feels the increasingly sharp bites of panic. The youth leader feels that the Manager lacks respect. He shouts, 'Do you want to live or die fat man?' In this moment, as short as a click of the fingers or as long as eternity, the birds stop singing, the sounds of traffic recede into silence, all activity ceases. There's only this moment.

The Manager begins to cry, 'I have a wife and three children. I pay school fees for my maid and gardener's children. I am a good man.' He repeats more slowly, as if to himself, 'I am a good man.'

The youth leader laughs, 'This fat white man is a good man!' The crowd of youth laughs loudly and forms a circle around him. Each youth sings, as they take turns kicking and slapping him, 'The fat white man is a good man!'

The sound of cars, engines growling at high acceleration, wheels turning, can be heard in the distance. Three cars shriek up Main Street, on a sunny day before tea-time in Gweru. They expertly glide into the parking bay. From the khaki-coloured army truck jump two rows of fully armed soldiers, bayonets glittering in the winter sunlight. From the two jeeps emerge more soldiers with truncheons and riot gear. And last, with a waddling stride, comes a man wearing an impressive khaki uniform with three rows of medals advertising his accomplishments. He has a barrel chest and a belly to match; a dark brown leather gun holster at his hip. His uniform is a work of precision: knife-edge creases and a flawlessly ironed uniform jacket. Middle aged, he is still strikingly handsome.

The two rows of soldiers march into the Mercedes dealership with speed and discipline, taking up positions at all exits, gun pressed to shoulder and finger on the trigger, ready. The other soldiers follow. They lower the visors of their riot helmets and have their truncheons raised. The youth continue kicking and slapping the manager, oblivious to the activity around them. 'Here's something to help you, fat white man,' says another youth. Cackling, he gives the Manager a good kick in the rear end which propels him several metres across the floor. The other youth cheer and applaud appreciatively. 'Ronaldo,' one shouts. 'No, it's Messi!' the other shouts. They all laugh. 'The only white man you can trust is a dead white man!' They all start to clap in rhythm repeating this phrase over and over again, like a mantra.

The youth hear a distant knock on the door. The man in uniform with three rows of medals is knocking on the front door with the butt of his gun. It is a beautiful weapon catching the sunlight on its golden flanks, the top adorned with diamonds stretching down the length of the barrel.

'These cars are already paid for. Come back next week,' one of the youth shouts, not looking at the man at the door. The youth is preoccupied with the Manager, waiting for him to rise to his knees so he can take another kick at his backside. The army officer walks purposefully into the centre of the room and places his gun to the temple of the young man who is waiting for the Manager to rise up on all fours. The youth turns angrily toward the source of his pain, 'What the fu…!' Then he recognises the man in uniform. 'General Muvudzi!' he stammers in alarm. 'General Muvudzi!' the rest of the youth exclaim in terror.

The youth brigade looks at the soldiers blocking the doors, bayonets pointed in their direction. They see more soldiers with riot helmets on and batons raised. The General now speaks, 'You have two minutes to vacate the premises. Any stragglers will be shot and buried in an unmarked grave.'

'Weapons to the ready,' the General orders. The soldiers unlatch the safety mechanism of their automatic rifles, the sound of multiple clicks like gun shots. Each of the soldiers centres their rifle sight on their chosen target. The General takes his gun, the gleaming gold exterior evoking dreams of unlimited wealth and the good life, and places it within arm's reach on the Manager's desk. The onlookers don't know what he will do next and inhale sharply. He smiles and looks at his watch. 'On your marks, get ready!' he announces. 'Go,' he says quietly.

Chaos ensues. Youths jump out of Mercedes, like termites scurrying from a termite mound which someone has accidentally kicked; others try to run to the exit doors only to be blocked and beaten by soldiers stationed there. Some smash through the plate glass window where white letters announce 'Dynamo Motors'. The discordant sound of glass breaking fills the air. There is screaming, yelling, and blood.

Looking over the heads of the soldiers, observing the scene, slender and well dressed, in tight fitting black jeans and a white shirt, is the kombi driver. He is looking at the General's gun. He's mesmerized by the General's gun. Two youth rugby tackle a soldier knocking him down, a victory, before six other army men pile on top of them, batons beating a bass rhythm to the screams.

At that moment a soldier comes barreling through to help his comrades, pushing the kombi driver into the showroom, a scene of mayhem. Several youth grab him, begging him to take them to his kombi, but he keeps running searching for a safe exit, darting in between the Mercs.

Then, he sees the gun, shimmering amidst the pulses of the showroom's fluorescent lights. He moves as if in slow motion, fascinated by the sparkle of the gun barrel as the diamonds reflect the light. They remind him of his mother's gold sequined dress glinting in the light of the sitting room as she danced. He feels the power of the gun in his blood. With this gun he would set all men free. He runs towards what he seeks, skirting around the corner of a life-size image of an African woman in a pink bikini draped over a silver Mercedes. She is smiling in the direction of the Manager's desk.

The General is entertained by the chaos. He remembers the words of his Chief Commander, 'Let the guns speak.' One minute has elapsed. He walks over to a soldier, points to the youth brigade leader and whispers, 'Shoot him!' Several bullets whoosh through the air and thump into the young leader, the impact slamming him into a wall. He collapses onto the floor. This event increases the activity level in the room.

Mr Mpofu, the elderly tea-boy, looks out from the kitchen and sees the General's gun. He sucks in his breath, imagining himself in the general's uniform. He pictures all the respectful ranks of soldiers in straight lines and crisp uniforms, ready for dress parade. He imagines what he would tell them to do. He imagines using the gun. Realising what he must do, Mr Mpofu wheels out the tea cart among the bullets and bodies falling. Nothing touches him. On the cart, there is a large tea cosy with nothing underneath it.

Across the room, one soldier in particular has his eye on the General's gun, while the rest of him rifle butts every youth who tries to make it past him. He's thinking how much he could sell that gun for. The Marange diamonds on the barrel are still worth a fortune. He could finally afford to feed his family, rather than live on bread and tea, while he waits for the monthly paycheck which always comes late. He's a soldier with a mission.

Time passes. The General's watch now indicates one minute and fifty seconds and the General is becoming bored. He motions to his men to begin shooting. There is still a group of youths determined to retrieve something of value, their eyes drawn to the Mercedes silver insignia rising proudly from the bonnet of every car. Suddenly, their bodies explode, lumps of flesh ricocheting off the walls.

It is over. He's unhurt. The Manager steps out of the metal utility closet where they keep the microfibre polishing cloths that Dynamo Motors proudly gives each customer to maintain the sheen of their new vehicles. He wants to shoot the asshole who beat him up. Shoot him in the butt. With a gun like that he could finally get some respect, quit this stupid job and make things happen. All he can think about is the gun.

During this pause in the atrocities, the kombi driver sees his opportunity and sprints to the back room, which is small with a two-plate electric stove, a half full box of Tanganda tea, and a Defy white refrigerator. The back door is open and he runs out into the daylight, into freedom.

The soldiers haul off those still living to jail. Who knows when they will be released? Who knows if anyone will ever know they've been thrown in jail? If they have connections to people in power, they will be out within a day or two, ready to rejoin the Youth Brigade.

The General looks around the room with satisfaction and orders his men to remove the bodies and dump them into the truck. Then he turns to the Manager and says, 'In the beginning you whites fought against this Indigenisation Act that requires a fifty-one percent partnership with Zimbabweans. Now you can see that it's a good thing. Sir, tell your boss that I work hard for my fifty-one percent. Kindly send the profit check by the end of the month.'

Returning to the Manager's desk he reaches for his gun. His hand closes on air. 'Where is my gun?' he bellows. The soldiers look at each other, baffled. 'Find my gun, now!' the General shouts. The men begin to look in all the places a gun might fall in the heat of battle, pushing aside any body parts that might obscure the gun from view.

The kombi driver is breathing hard from what he has witnessed in the last two minutes of his life. Running to the kombi, parked nearby in a side alley, he removes a crumpled knapsack from under the seat. He pulls out a casual but fashionable dress, flat women's shoes, a padded bra and make-up. He quickly begins to change. His legs are smooth and hairless. The dress falls, appropriately, just below the knee and shows off the curves of the padded bra. He puts on the wig, secures it, and takes one last look at himself in the rear view mirror before closing and locking the kombi. The sun illuminates the silver lettering on the windscreen which proclaims, '*God Knows*'. She smiles, takes out a tissue and wipes a bit of lipstick from her front tooth. There is considerable room between her flat chest and where the padding of the bra begins.

The General will have his gun. It is the backbone of this country. But they cannot find the gun. In all his years of fighting, even during post-independence, vanquishing the opposition, ensuring peace in this land, the General always had the gun by his side. It has never left him. The golden gun was a gift from his most trusted soldiers, honouring his years of leadership. He added the Marange diamonds when he was put in charge of security for the mine. This gun gave him a second honeymoon when he returned from two years in the DRC, co-ordinating military operations. His marriage had cooled and grown distant over those years. But when he showed his wife his golden gun, the barrel highlighted with diamonds, she fell in love with it and with him, again. In the bedroom, she would twirl the gun while seductively moving her hips. He must have that gun!

The General is whipping himself into a fury. And then, he remembers how the Manager had been captivated by his gun. Like a hungry man staring at food that he has no money to buy. He faces the Manager and looks him in the eye for several long seconds. 'Where's my gun!' he demands. The Manager does not flinch from his gaze. He orders his soldiers to search him. 'Where's my gun?' he repeats with increasing anger. The General receives no response, just the unflinching gaze of the Manager. 'You can usually trust a white man,' he thinks but his intuition tells him that if this man doesn't have the gun, he knows who took it. 'Handcuff him to the jeep,' he commands his soldiers.

As the soldiers roughly escort him from the showroom, the Manager halts in front of the General, 'What has this country done to us?' he says with a mixture of vehemence and bewilderment. Laughing, the General replies, 'You have it all wrong. What has this country done to you? Not us! I'm doing very well, thank you.' Thinking about who he will interrogate next, the General walks away.

Mr Mpofu, the tea-boy, observes the proceedings with an impassive face, hopeful that the General will never find the answer. The tea-boy has had enough. He calmly exits Dynamo Motors. He will not be making tea there anytime soon, he thinks to himself.

The soldier who had his eye on the General's gun is happy. He hums as he drags deceased members of the Youth Brigade from the car dealership and throws them into the truck.

The army continues to investigate, stopping and searching passers-by and kicking in the doors of various houses and flats in the neighbourhood. They carefully search all the restaurants and cafes in the area and anyone who'd stood watching the events that transpired at Dynamo Motors is dragged into the interrogation room.

The kombi driver, Tafadzwa, or Tati, as her transgender friends call her, walks leisurely down Fifth Street, her hips lilting in the sunlight. Tati doesn't want to draw attention to herself, but she has a lithe beauty that men notice. She makes a right turn to end on Chitepo Avenue, arriving at a rather dilapidated building. There's the bass sound of disco music emanating from three floors above. Tati begins to climb the stairs to the tiny flat. The lift has long ago stopped functioning.

There's a lively party going on at Tati's flat, though it is only two in the afternoon. A strobe light reflects off a red disco ball, creating the effect of crimson lightning. All her friends are there. Some have done a poor job shaving their faces, others have carelessly applied their make-up (Tati makes a note to sit them down for a make-over lesson), but they're all in their best party dresses so their dereliction can be excused. Some are slinky, some are bony, some are overly muscular, but they're all women. They revel in their gender. Some skitter across the dance floor on high heels, while others perform highly sexual moves.

Tati walks over to the group gathered in the lounge. She sits down. Removing an object from the space between her chest and her bra, Tati shows all her friends – the gun. It is surprisingly light for a weapon. One woman strokes the barrel, loving its smoothness. She compares the gun to the male organ which they all possess. 'I would much rather have the gun! And what I could do with those diamonds!' she says marvelling. Another woman puts out her hands, almost in supplication. The gun, a holy item, is placed in her two palms. She smells it, then licks the barrel, to screams of delight from the other women. They are cheering and effortlessly hoist Tati onto their shoulders while she swings the gun around and around in circles.

They're dancing. 'I got the power!' they sing. They are delirious with pleasure and laughter, singing louder and louder. They all worship the gun. There's a knock on the door. There is a volley of strong knocks on the door. There is the crunching sound of wood being splintered by rifle butts. Tati keeps dancing. They all keep dancing. All her friends singing together, 'I got the power!'

Bob liked Pinstripes

Sam Brakarsh

It had a sphere about the size of a soccer ball perched on top of a twenty-centimeter cylinder which, in some way, was connected to something encased by a suit. It smiled. Its name was Bob. He was an insurance broker.

It would, in fact, be more accurate to say that he looked as if he should be wearing a suit. He had a gut that seemed just prominent enough to place the appropriate amount of tension on the blue buttons at the front of a blazer; and calves that, in the right light, one might go so far as to say looked muscular in pinstripes. Bob liked pinstripes. He liked the way they fell straight down the suit when it hung in his closet but were forced to curve elegantly around his body when he wore them. It was a curve that showed a man who did not like his job but had decided a long time ago that the way to compensate was to enjoy life all the more. He smiled.

In this case he was not wearing pinstripes. He was wearing shorts. Shorts that doubled as a swimming costume. And had little green palm trees and little yellow pineapples printed on a red material. He had a red Coca Cola T-shirt to match. He wore a toupée that had the most extraordinary ability to show, without a doubt, that the hair was not coming out of his head. This issue was probably not helped by the fact that the toupée was brown and all the other hair on his body was black.

He wore sandals in the colours of the Brazilian flag. He was not in Brazil. He was at his three-year-old's birthday party on the beach.

Jane. Was Bob's wife. And dead. She was happy. She liked the way that nothingness felt on her skin. Or at least that's what Bob told himself. She had died giving birth to Sarai their daughter. It was a 'C' section. The operation had gone fine. Nobody had made any mistakes, she just died. 'Sometimes it happens,' the doctor had told him. Bob was not an emotional person when it came to sadness. Bob only ever felt happiness... Or nothing. It was nothing that happened on the day that his wife died. Bob very quickly got rid of nothing and became happy again. He treated his wife's death like a nine-to-five job – something you just had to deal with.

Sarai liked her father but she didn't like pinstripes; she liked playing with sand, hence the birthday party on the beach. Sarai wore a little pink dress with polka dots, not pinstripes. She had grown up loved, loved before nine and loved after five. The rest of the time she was just liked. Bob let her play at a daycare while he was at work. It was the friends that she made there who liked her very much and formed the body of guests at the beach party. Being on the beach made all the guests like Sarai even more, but no one there really liked Bob at this point, not even Sarai. This may or may not be related to the fact that Bob was shovelling sand with their favourite blue bucket.

The air tinkled in Bob's ears. A few molecules missed his ears and hit his head. He didn't notice them much. It was the tinkling of childish joy. A truck came to a stop at the edge of the road at the point where the city stopped and the beach started. Bob stood up with purpose and walked with determination towards the truck. Anyone watching him would have been concerned about what would happen next. On his way to the truck, Bob carefully placed the blue bucket beside Sarai's right knee. It was his favourite blue bucket. Sarai looked up at him with a delighted, half-toothed grin. He loved Sarai very much. Not because she reminded him of Jane but because she reminded him of something completely unique. Bob smiled back at her.

'I'll be back in a sec, I promise.' Sarai wasn't worried. She was worried the first time he'd said that to her when he left the house at 8:30 in the morning, but he always came back. Bob stroked her hair one last time before turning and walking purposefully away. A Coca Cola T-shirt and swimming trunks with little green palm trees and little yellow pineapples on it had never been seen to move with more purpose. Without a weakening in his resolve he stepped up to the truck and anxiously asked, 'What flavours do you have?' The man answered with a half smile,

'Strawberry and vanilla.'

'Ah,' Bob said wincing, 'No chocolate?'

'And chocolate,' said the ice-cream man. Bob grinned. He really liked chocolate ice-cream.

'Could I please have four vanillas and three strawberries.' Bob knew what all the kids' favourite flavours were. There were seven kids. He then added, 'And three chocolates.' There was one Bob. He smiled sheepishly. As the man stuffed the balls of ice-cream into pale orange cones, a ripping noise came from one of Bob's Velcro pockets where he kept his money. He only wore the swimming costume as 'beach etiquette'. He didn't plan on actually getting wet. He paid the ice-cream man, took all the cones in a big embrace and started walking back to the children. He liked the feeling of the sand pushing through his toes on the beach, but in this case he was wearing sandals, so he kicked them off. Every child gave his knee a little hug before grabbing at their cone. When James grabbed at his vanilla, the cone and ice-cream separated and both ended up in the sand, crusted by the little gold grains. James looked at it longingly, contemplating whether it was still worth consumption. Bob smiled and handed him a chocolate cone; he knew James also liked chocolate. The ice-cream man watched them.

His name was Wilfred; he liked children. He didn't have any children, but he liked them. That's why he became an ice-cream man. He liked it when children came to order ice-creams themselves. He would usually serve them regardless of whether or not they could pay. His favourite flavour was caramel, but he didn't really like ice-cream. He had always wanted to be a professional soccer player but was very clumsy and tripped going up some stairs, breaking a little bone in his foot. It was still sore to kick things. Wilfred was very logically minded and had a bachelor's degree in marine biology. He was not logical enough to realize that he wouldn't be able to find work after graduating from his small university. He had tried for a while but when he married Diana, she started getting fed up with supporting him so he took a job as an ice-cream man. He made sure that he had a route where he could watch the ocean. Diana never told him that he should become an ice-cream man, he'd just become one. They'd been married for seven years; he'd been an ice-cream man for six. They lived in a small apartment an hours' drive from the ocean and in a years' time they were planning on selling it and buying an even smaller one on the beach.

Bob sat down on the beach next to Sarai and hugged her. An unusually large wave fell onto the sand and forced its way up the slope, stretching until it was able to clean Bob's feet. Sarai poked the water with her toe just before it started retreating back to the ocean, preparing itself for another attempt to wet Bob's swimming costume for the very first time in the three years that he had owned it. James and Sarai's other friends continued digging holes in the sand. James quickly jerked his head upwards, squinting into the sun because he heard the sound of a jet flying overhead. James liked big things; James liked loud things; James liked flying things; hence, James really liked jet planes. His eyes walked all over the sky, carefully sidestepping the glaring sun, in desperate pursuit of his beloved jet, which seemed to be growing louder and louder. A few unsatisfying moments later James realised that the noise wasn't a jet at all, it was only the ocean which had decided to roar especially loudly to tease him. In his frustration, he hurled a clump of wet sand at the sea. It felt good, so he picked up another clump.

Bob looked out at the water in the orangey haze. There was the most elegant looking wave forming on the horizon behind an average-sized cruise ship. He wished he'd brought his camera. Sarai squirmed out of her father's arms and joined her friends in the gleeful game of throwing clumps of wet sand into the water. Bob threw his gaze back at the horizon. He rarely ever got to appreciate nature, but he did now. Bob was astonished at how high the wave lifted the cruise ship and he very quickly concluded that it was a brilliant illusion of the golden air. There was a shriek as one of the clumps of sand that Sarai was about to throw revealed the surprise of small crab. She carefully placed the clump back on the beach and eagerly scooped up a new, crabless one.

Bob's smile quickly faded as he saw the average-sized cruise ship topple off the wave. He pulled himself to his feet, reaching for the arms of the children, desperately trying to bring them under his control. They were laughing hysterically in anticipation of the tickle that always followed being pursued by Bob. Sarai wasn't laughing or running away from her father. She knew his tickle face and this wasn't it. She was frightened. Bob yanked at Sarai's hand hard enough that the sand fell out of her closed fist. The other children noticed Bob's desperation for the first time, and allowed themselves to be captured. They were now scared. They weren't quite sure why they were scared, but they felt that they should be. Bob started dragging them away from the receding tide. He ran past the ice-cream truck, pulling Sarai and her friends faster and faster down the streets. The wave continued to push its way through the water.

Wilfred didn't start the engine of the ice-cream truck or look panicked in any way. He looked deeply sad as he pressed the button to end the phone call he had just had with Diana. Wilfred knew enough about the ocean to understand that he couldn't escape the wave that was approaching. So he watched it.

The roar grew louder.

Wilfred liked children.

Sarai liked sand.

James liked vanilla ice-cream but if it was not available also thoroughly enjoyed chocolate.

Bob liked pinstripes.

Jane liked the feeling of nothingness.

A Late Arrival

Godess Bvukutwa

Their tired eyes searched the road repeatedly. Their ears yearned for any sound, any sound at all that could tingle and excite the boredom which was now threatening to wear them down. Not that the sun's mercenary blades were not doing a good job of wearing them out. No. But still they waited. They had to wait. The acid-inspired music in their stomachs commanded them to wait. After all, they had witnessed with their very eyes as Toringepi massacred the bull. So they mopped their foreheads, licked their dry lips and waited.

Some of them muttered and grumbled beneath their breaths so others wouldn't hear. Some of the men played drafts under the gum trees that the old German missionary had planted. A pity he was gone now. *Mxeem.* I saw Sekuru Gava scratching his bald head as if there was still hair on it. And I spotted Ma'Khumalo, that Ndebele woman who was part of the dancing team, rubbing her eyes as if they were sore. And just by the roadside, Nomore was walking about with his hands in the front pockets of his washed-out jeans, which I swore I'd seen his friend Jojo wearing just the day before.

And then, just as I began to yawn, my mouth wide open, my mother, who was seated next to my sister, Chido, gave me a stern look; then someone shouted something and we all looked towards the noise, our hearts thumping. Sure enough, there was dust in the distance, which even the partially blind Sekuru Gava couldn't deny. The MP had arrived and I saw Ma'Khumalo stand up and start to shake her waist in preparation for the dance.

VaMusonyori and VaChisveru visibly started to feel important as they drew on their discarded, worn-out blazers, and began moving their wooden stools from under the shade of the gum trees to the front of the crowd. I could see the inscription on VaMusonyori's stool: 'Mhofu yeMukono', and I thought, 'my father made those'. VaMusonyori and VaChisveru were two of the leaders, so we all expected them to move to the front. I saw VaChisveru's younger wife feigning nonchalance as her husband moved forward, but we all knew that she was secretly beaming with pride like a tower light in the city. Not every woman's husband sat in front with the MP when he came on one of his rare visits. I nudged my sister with my elbow to look at Mai Chisveru and we giggled maliciously behind our work-gnawed hands. The dust in the distance we could all see, and a woman wearing a white doek carelessly on her head suddenly erupted into a dangerously soulful song. Her eyes were closed, and she was bobbing her head up and down as if she was drunk with the spirit or something. 'She must be from Mwazha apostolic sect,' I thought.

I could now smell Toringepi's bull boiling in the drum from where I was. And that was the very second I saw The Boys coming out of the bushes that hid Chazezesa Secondary school to our right. Everyone saw them, The Boys. I felt my heart capsize and then sink, and sink, as fear rose up right up to my throat and l felt it choking me, gathering heat in my neck and face. I saw the same fear in Chido my sister's eyes, and in the eyes of the sunburnt faces around us. I saw VaMusonyori unconsciously move his stool backwards, nearly upsetting it, his eyes focusing on The Boys like a magnet. The Boys moved in on the crowd that had now gone deathly quiet except for Rogo who was shouting at them in an unsettling show of bravery. But then Rogo, we all knew, was not right in his mind at times, especially when the moon was full.

There were about twelve of them and they were unsuccessfully hiding long, thin branches of the German missionary's gum trees behind their backs. They encircled us like a pack of hyenas moving in on its prey. The one who came closest to where we were seated had huge patches of sweat under his black T-shirt, his eyes were bloodshot and he was sucking on a maroon-coloured lollipop.

We knew they were The Boys but we did not know them. We knew them because of the whispering voices from other areas, that they were modern day guerrillas of the liberation war. They lived in the bush and survived on people's cattle, goats, grain and virgins. Yes, we had heard that they took the girls they fancied in the villages as theirs. They played hide and seek with the people, appearing by night and disappearing like the dew with daybreak. Some villagers were purported to have pointed them out at beer halls, laughing: guffaws of laughter, like landlords on their property, drinking beer as if it was free, dancing unknown dances from foreign places and pinching the plump buttocks of the village maidens. They had ears on the very ground the villagers ploughed every November, ears in the sweet air smelling of rain, cow dung and *hute,* ears at the bus stops marked by useless pieces of zinc on which was written something like, 'Mushayavanhu Bus Stop' with a piece of charcoal and posted onto the trunk of a Munhondo tree. They had ears everywhere the voices had said in harsh whispers. Even in churches. That is why our very own German missionary had left, they said. *Mxeem,* such a pity he was gone, they said, shaking their heads from side to side countless times. It was he who had helped to complete the Form 1 and Form 2 classroom blocks that termites had begun to feed on, on seeing the school's abandonment years ago. Another heartfelt *mxeem.* They had eyes too. And fists. And hands that could hold a handmade *sjambok* very well. And feet that liked wearing boots. Strong, black leather boots which could stamp on you mercilessly, until your cries became hoarse, became whimpers, became non-existent. Their feet liked wearing boots just like the feet of the comrades during the war of liberation. Boots that stomped the ground and chased away the sand to the sides in fear. Boots that made the grass gasp and run the other way as the boots thudded their way into the villages in the still of the night, and everyone pretended to be asleep as they smelt the smell of dry grass burning; dry grass which in daylight had been someone's thatch on someone's hut. As they heard the desperate, begging wails of women; the loud, defenceless howls of their men; the confused cries of their children and the feverish barking of their dogs. They pretended to be asleep. They pretended to be asleep as the boots thudded their way back into the bush. Sometimes accompanied with laughter, sometimes with harsh, angry voices, and sometimes by silence. A silence that would hush and haunt the entire village for many sunrises afterwards.

So we knew The Boys but we did not know them. We did not know them because they were always from somewhere else. The voices said they got boys from somewhere across the country to go to unfamiliar areas. Anyone could do anything far from the place where their umbilical cord was cut and buried. Far from their mother's eyes. Some said they were given lots of money and some said brown barrels of Chibuku beer were bought for them along with a plate of sadza and that was it. But, what we all agreed with the voices was that they were given power beyond us simple villagers' wildest imaginations.

Why was the MP's entourage not getting any nearer? The dust in the distance was closer I noted just as the one who looked like the leader of The Boys leapt onto a stool at the front. He was wearing black and red. Black pants and a black, roughly cut vest. A hurriedly folded dirty red bandanna concealed the top of his ears. Bulging muscles were screaming to be let out of the thin vest. And when he opened his mouth, thunder escaped along with threatening spits of saliva through clenched cigarette-stained teeth. The pounding of my heart punctuated my fear through my green and brown blouse.

'*Makadini vagari vemuno maRugare.*'

We muttered in reply to his greeting in unison. The worry and tension in this harmony was sad. So sad that he laughed. He looked much younger, when he laughed. He sure was not a day older than thirty.

'My name is Jack Nyikainotakaifira Munetsi. You do not know me but, by the time we are done, I am sure we will be knowing each other's totems. We are here to do a job. Word came to our ears where we were about you people from Rugare. About how you totally disregard authority and do exactly what you want. *Madiro aGeorginah chaiwo,* when this country is at stake. When this country is like a piece of meat that everybody wants and, if we are not careful, it will be taken and eaten by other people, yet it was what we fought for in the war of liberation. You see...' He stopped a bit and shook his head, his face showing disdain and consternation in anticipation of what he was about to say. He raised his right hand for emphasis. 'You see, I do not understand you people,' he stopped again, swallowing saliva, and put down his hand with great force. 'You said you wanted freedom from white colonial rule. We heard you. And we left our homes, our parents, our warm beds with our wives, to go and live in the bush with snakes as companions, Smith's bullets as lullabies and AK47s as pillows. And every day, we struggled to give you all the freedom you yearned for. *Mxeem!*' he clicked his tongue exaggeratedly. '*Shame maningisterek.*

'And now this is what we get from you. Disloyalty. Disloyalty to the cause of the liberation struggle. Have you forgotten this? Have you forgotten the reason why we are all here today, free..., free as a prostitute in the avenues of Harare. Well-fed too, like a child on Christmas Day. And our children are getting educated and speaking English better than the Queen herself. *Ha ha ha.* But still, that is not enough. You still want to cling to the white man like leeches on a cow's hide. You yearn and beg to be colonised again like former slaves who do not know what to do with themselves after being set free from the master, and so they wish to go into captivity again. So we want these traitors here in Rugare to be an example to all of you, these sell-outs that don't know that the gains of the liberation war have to be protected at all costs.'

I was seething inside from the moment Comrade Jack Munetsi had spoken about education. I wanted to stand up and shout and scream about our school Chazezesa Secondary, why it still had only two classroom blocks and one teacher's house. Where was the money that had been donated by the German priest Father Hausberg to build the Form 3 and Form 4 blocks and other teacher's houses? Had he not gone to Bonn, his home town, to beg his family and friends to give money for the school just as he had done years back to bring a doctor for the mission hospital? Had he not said his brother, a farmer, had had to sell two of his heifers to contribute to the school? He had come back triumphant and we had sung songs and lifted his fat self up. Ma'Khumalo and her girls had almost danced their waists off and the Chief, the Headman and the Sabhukus had smiled toothless smiles all day long into the camera that Vhurumu had whipped out of his bag; and Nomore had snapped and snapped photos all day like somebody was paying him. Everyone was there and it had been a merry day. And then days passed like sand through an hour glass, as the cliché goes. And then weeks passed. But nothing happened. The bricks that we had begun to make as a village were abandoned and soon the weather weathered them. Months passed and still only the termites grew.

Voices began to whisper, as they usually do, that the leaders of the People's Party, our party in Rugare, had gone nicodemously to seek audience with Father Hausberg. They told him that they wanted to be in charge of the school project because the word that was doing rounds in the high offices was that the money had come from Western detractors who wanted to turn the hearts of the people against the party of the people. They demanded the money from him and said they would lead the classroom project in order to calm down the boiling blood of the people in the high offices. So Father Hausberg gave them some of the money, albeit hesitantly. And still nothing happened. No builders came to dig foundations or measure any measurements. But soon enough, the voices had said, the nicodemous visitors wanted the rest of the money that 'they had sent him to look for in his home country.' They accused him of getting money abroad using pitiful photos of African children and then keeping the money for himself. When the old missionary remained adamant, rumours were spread that he was indeed an agent of the West whose agenda was to turn the people against the People's Party. One day he woke up and his dog Ruramai had been slain and the decapitated body placed on his doorstep. They began hounding him even in church and during prayers; they would loudly say prayers about not wanting to be forced to do things they didn't want to do. He gave them the money and begged them to use it for the classrooms. In weeks, Father Hausberg's greyish hair had grown white, his slouch had worsened and the wrinkles on his face seemed to have grown deeper. He did not stay for long after that.

And still, not a suspicion of a classroom was even remotely built. Just that Nehosho bought a second-hand truck and began charging people to ferry their tobacco bales to the city. He couldn't drive, so he hired Nomore's friend Jojo to do the job and Nomore was his assistant. That was why the two boys now had money to flash about, get drunk and pester us girls. VaMudzimu extended his house and painted it cream and maroon. It was the most beautiful house in all the villages. A few other people all of whom were coincidentally in the top echelons of the party in Rugare began showing signs of wealth. Some bought carts, cattle and some started small businesses. And the rest of us…, well, we were in awe, stupefied, helpless awe. Hopes of attending school close by for Form 3 and 4 were washed away in the Chikware River that we now had to cross every sunrise and sunset, walking the ten kilometre distance to Chikware Secondary School in Gambiza village. We always arrived tired and hungry and sometimes late. I dozed in class countless times because we also got home late and I had to help with the chores and then do homework by the firelight, if I hadn't fallen asleep already. Some students dropped out especially during the rainy season when the Chikware River filled up and became too dangerous to cross.

'So I have a list here with me. Of the traitors. You shall come up here and queue in the order that I call you and my boys here will make examples of you to everyone else,' said Comrade Jack Munetsi

And he began calling out names just like a prison roll call, one by one. The headmaster of Chazezesa Secondary School topped the list, followed by most of his teachers and the nurses and staff of the mission hospital, and Ma'Khumalo; and Vhurumu, the grocer, who of course wasn't there. He was never there. Munya the boy I dreamed about who was on vacation from the university and his friend Rony. Tecla who was the storekeeper in Vhurumu's Minimarket and Take-Away, as well as her mother who sold fruits and vegetables at the shops. The great farmer, VaHondongwi and his two sons. Our parish chairperson and the quiet woman who sometimes started songs in church. And lastly our father, the village carpenter. Tears let themselves out of my eyes and I prayed silently for the dust that was escorting the Member of Parliament to get to the rally faster. Tecla began to cry and the headmaster with a quivering voice tried to reason with The Boys whilst wearing his most diplomatic face but, alas, it was a waste of both quivers and breathe. Bending down low, he was whipped on his backside with a skinned gum tree branch and he howled like the small boys he was used to beating up at school.

I saw in a blur caused by the tears flooding my eyes, Ma'Khumalo trying to negotiate something. At first Comrade Jack brushed her aside like a fly irritatingly interrupting his meal, and then he suddenly took interest when she continued saying something. I then saw their blurred shapes leaving the crowd, towards the gum trees where they disappeared from sight.

'Do you think he will cry,' I asked Chido when it was almost our father's turn to receive the thirty-five lashes on his behind.

'I don't know,' she said fighting back her tears. But our mother, to Chido's right, wasn't trying to hide her tears and allowed them to flow quietly down her cheeks.

Thankfully, he did not howl like the headmaster had done. With each gum tree stroke he groaned and grunted between tightly clenched teeth. By the time they were done, we were all sobbing quite pitifully.

Comrade Jack Munetsi emerged from the trees whistling. He whispered something to one of The Boys and the Boy walked very fast to the gum trees where Jack Munetsi had just emerged.

One after the other, Boy after Boy went behind the gum trees where Ma'Khumalo was still to re-emerge.

Ma'Khumalo did not dance that day when later the MP's entourage finally arrived with fanfare. In fact, I never saw Ma'Khumalo dance again. Some church women carried Ma'Khumalo to the hospital after she was found still lying in the gum trees when they came looking for her. They said, she had a blank look on her face that frightened them.

The cloud of dust that had momentarily flown out of the window of our thought faculties arrived now as if out of nowhere. The boys hurriedly disappeared into the bushes, the way they had come, just after Comrade Jack Munetsi had told us to carry on as normal, as if nothing had happened. But, alas, it was not the MP who got out of the big vehicle that was revealed to us slowly as the dust settled. It was a four-wheel drive, a majestic, gleaming silver vehicle with a powerful engine drone. The unmistakable pot belly belonging to Vhurumu showed itself first before its owner jumped out of the vehicle in apparent haste and began walking towards the dismal crowd. Vhurumu was a troublesome character. Everyone knew this. It was even evident in his facial features. His eyes were shifty, never seeming able to stay in one place. Shifting here, shifting there, every few seconds. His sharp pointed nose and his thin lips always seemed to conspire with each other, as if they knew something you did not. The smattering of a beard above his upper lip also seemed to be part of this conspiracy. It moved this way and that way whenever he spoke, revealing teeth that were in a sort of dance in his mouth. Some were facing east, some south. Some were shorter, some longer. It was hard to believe anything that came out of his mouth when his whole visage made it seem like a joke. He was like a human version of Tsuro, the hare in the *Tsuro naGudo* folktales. He was short and carried with him everywhere, two things: his pot belly, well tucked into his trousers, and a brown leather handheld bag that always raised an eyebrow or two as to what it contained. Was it money? Was it important documents from the city to which he was always disappearing? Was it some party regalia belonging to the political party whose T-shirts he was wont to wear when he felt like it?

To be seen talking to Vhurumu was looking for trouble. Just as now. As he walked towards the crowd, everyone wanted to know what he wanted, yet most people's eyes shied away from him. It was as if just looking at him would attract some of the guilt, which the community had found Vhurumu to hold, on unclear charges. What did he want now, this trouble maker? I could almost hear the thought machinery working laboriously in many a mind. Hadn't he caused enough pain and destruction already? Isn't he the one who had caused The Boys to come?

Yes, it was true. The voices had begun whispering many half moons ago. Of the secret meetings that were taking place in the backroom of Vhurumu's Minimarket and Restaurant. The voices said, a lot of men were involved in these secret meetings as well as some daring women. What they discussed in the shadows of darkness, even the voices were yet to know. But what they knew was the People's Party leaders were not part of the invited guests to Vhurumu's late night meetings. No. The Almighty Nehosho wasn't there. Neither was vaMudzimu or Mr Murefu. The meetings were at times chaired by Tecla's mother, the fruit and vegetable vendor, and this has made a lot of people laugh. What could old Mai Tecla know, except about charging people one and two rand coins? Ha ha ha. It was a joke. No one believed it and everyone dismissed the voices' insistence that it was the truth. But apparently not every one dismissed the voices, as was evidenced by Comrade Munetsi's list. Everyone who was on it had been whispered about by the voices as having attended at least some of Vhurumu's midnight meetings.

Vhurumu walked up front and began talking. He looked a bit different, somehow. I leaned forward to get a closer look and I swore I saw tears in the man's eyes, precariously on the verge of falling. It was this that made everyone even consider listening to him. And his first words, 'I'm sorry. I am so sorry. I hope you will find it in your hearts to forgive me one day. I know what has just taken place and I take the blame because of the meetings everyone knew we were having in my store. I am aware of what has happened because just as I was coming from Harare, I stopped by at Murambadoro Growth Point about forty-five kilometres from here. And there, I saw the MP's motorcade, which was also parked at the growth point. I was surprised: why were they lounging around there, when they had a rally here? They were there drinking drinks and talking and laughing loudly. And guess who I saw in the midst of all this, whispering words in the MP's ear?' He stopped for a while shaking his head and then continued. 'It was Jack Munetsi.'

Everyone gasped not knowing whether to believe Vhurumu or not.

'I know Munetsi from way back. And I had heard of the business he's into and immediately I knew what was going to happen and I knew they would be gunning for me so I stayed at Murambadoro watching the MP and his buddies eating and drinking knowing that they had sent The Boys to do their dirty job for them. But when I saw them leave the growth point, that is when I took another route and drove here as fast as I could. '

'So … What are you saying with all this, Vhurumu? What are you asking us to do?' cried the distraught voice of Sekuru Gava.

'If you think I'm lying. Look here, I managed to take some photos.' He opened his brown leather bag and photos fell out as if they had been told to.

'I had them processed at Murambadoro,' he said as he passed around several photos of the just departed Cde Munetsi and some of The Boys with the MP that we were all still waiting for.

Vhurumu continued. 'I am now proposing that we all go to our homes and boycott this rally as a way of protest. If we remain here we are accepting such behaviour from people who are supposed to be our leaders.

'Look! Here they are. We have to act fast. Don't wait for the rally!'

Sure enough we saw the entourage that we'd all been waiting for all morning moving towards the venue. Vhurumu quickly left the front of the crowd; at his heels followed Tecla's mother, freshly beaten and limping in pain. The rest of us just sat there, as if frozen on our behinds, although, those of us who had been lashed were lying on the ground unmoving.

Vhurumu and Mai Tecla left soon afterwards after leaving a cloud of dust in their wake.

Vhurumu did not understand. Not only was Comrade Jack Munetsi's message still loud and fresh, but the villagers were tired and confused. They felt like a *chikweshe*, a handmade football which their children kicked back and forth from one makeshift goal post to another. The sun's mercenary blades had worn them down but still they waited. They had to wait. The acid inspired music in their stomachs commanded them to wait. After all they had witnessed with their very eyes as Toringepi massacred the bull. So they mopped their foreheads, licked their dry lips and waited.

Plenty Ways to Die in the Republic

Lawrence Hoba

Maki knows there are plenty other ways to die without being beaten to a pulp by an over-zealous mob of party youths. In fact, right now, this is one of the easiest ways to die in the republic. But, it's just too early in the morning to die stupidly and dishonourably like the *kachasu* drinkers who are sometimes picked up at daybreak, dead in dry sewer drains, drowned in their own vomit. One can always wait for the moment when all that can be done in a day is done. After all, it's the most principled thing to do in life – die when one is expected to die. When the time comes, one should just leave: allowing your spirit to linger, to hang around wanting to stay, well, that's plain inconvenient.

The Old Man doesn't care about what or what is not convenient. He has refused to die and it doesn't bother him that everything around him is collapsing and that everyone wants him dead. Maybe now that they say he died forty days ago, the longest he's ever been dead, he is finally dead. That's pretty scary because, as Maki knows, the truth is that no one really wants the Old Man dead; everyone is scared that the republic will just sink into the grave with him, the moment he's buried. Each time the Old Man has died, a part of the republic has died with him; but it's unlike him not to resurrect himself. And if he doesn't do it now, it may be the end of the republic, at least as they know it.

The Old Man's followers liken him to the Messiah, much to the exasperation of the Prophet who prefers to see himself as the sixth or seventh in the order of heaven, due to his miracle-making abilities. Maki, who has sworn that he does not care about the Old Man any more, runs to catch up with the group of Party crowd-pushers. They're coming anyway, and they sweep everything in their wake along with them. To try and avoid them now will be the surest way to the quickest ending that Maki has ever imagined.

By now the motley crowd consists of mainly adolescent youth reeking of sorrow-drowning illicit brews ranging from cane spirits to cough mixtures, children too young to understand politics and a few older looking men and women. They are singing, dancing and clapping to a cocktail of revolutionary songs booming from a new Party-colour-branded Hilux truck, travelling at human pace. Though seemingly calm, Maki knows it will not need much to electrify the gathering and turn it into a murderous rabble. Being a former crowd-pusher, he is all too well aware of this and has already resigned his fate to whatever this Saturday will bring.

But, as usual, he doesn't know what the cause of the current round-up is. Disconcerting for a man who used to be one of them. Outspoken at times, defiant at others, but mostly resolute about the revolutionary ideals that made his Party the right one, it had been widely expected that some day he would emerge as one of the young leaders. But one day he woke up and left it all behind him, even as they had told him that he was a reincarnation of the Old Man himself; a youth of great revolutionary promise.

***

Maki, who still has not seen anyone he knows among the leaders of the crowd-pushers, doesn't bother asking about today's call. He walks, glad that he chose to wear a decent pair of trousers and sandals when he left the house. As on most occasions, the trip to fetch water from the sewer-fed vlei a short distance from his home should have been uneventful; the only possible difficulty being a long queue of people similarly wanting to fetch water, which sometimes provoked fights about who should be first. He had not anticipated any excitement, at least not anytime soon, especially with the Old Man out of the country for the longest time ever, and rumoured to be dead. It was said that this time the Old Man had been flown out in the wee hours of the night, dead as a stone; flown on the same plane intended to take the national football team to a crucial World Cup qualifying match, which, of course, they didn't manage to play. It was said that those very few, who knew where they'd taken his body, had chosen to keep it to themselves – as always.

Of course, the rumour-mill went into overdrive until it finally entangled itself in its own guesses, so that no one could possibly know the truth – if they ever did. The only facts the rumour-mongers agreed on were that this was the Old Man's fifth death and that this was the longest he'd ever been dead, and that it could not be ascertained whether he would get out of it, as always, alive. The count was made ignoring the many other occasions when the state had refuted claims of his death, especially those when he died and rose again within a few hours. Taking those into account would have made the death record an unassailable nine.

'Who do we have here?' Maki is startled by someone shouting in his ear, obviously wanting the message to be his.

'It is I, the prodigal son.' He responds to the voice without turning. He knows it's Jabu, who's always insisted that Maki was lost the moment he chose the Prophet's church over the Party. Jabu is wearing new shoes and a new outfit, unlike anything Maki has previously seen. He dangles a set of car keys in front of his friend's face.

'What's the cause for today's call?' Maki shouts, snatching the keys from Jabu. 'And whose pocket did you rob?'

'In my father's house there are plenty of riches and no stealing. You just take what you want without giving anything in return,' Jabu shouts back, assuming the pose and tone of Maki's prophet. 'We're going to the airport. There's a surprise for everyone. Especially you!'

'I hope your airport surprise includes food,' Maki calls out above the growing din of revolutionary songs, dance and chatter. Not new to the phenomenon of the airport surprises, he knows that once the steadily growing crowd sucks one in, it does not spit you out until it has sapped all your energy and achieved its goal for the day. Not that he wouldn't mind a little adventure. He wishes he had eaten his leftover sadza when he woke up.

Noting the look of worry on Maki's face, Jabu spoke sombrely, 'and don't tell me your life-giving Prophet hasn't cured you of your diabetes, because otherwise you'll starve to death today.'

Maki grins uneasily and shakes his head. He cannot tell Jabu that he'd nearly died three weeks ago when the Prophet told him to throw away his meds because he'd said that Maki was healed.

They pass by a wall plastered with his Prophet's posters. He pats his friend on the shoulder and shouts, 'See what that poster says, "it is you my enemy who will die next Saturday night and I will be there to see it". Remember it will be the night of final judgement.'

'Ha ha ha ha,' Jabu laughs mockingly, 'you know only one person has the power to kill their enemies in this whole country. And it's not your Papa Prophet.'

Now as the two are walking towards the terminus, where Maki knows scores of buses will be waiting to take them to the airport, disappointment creeps over him. The younger children are chanting along, too excited to last the distance and sometimes getting in the way of the marchers. No one seems bothered about them. Maki loves it. At his new church the ushers are especially quick to yank children or adults out of the way of orderly choreographed movements.

Maki knows that Jabu may be right. Sometimes he watches youths gather in small groups, chasing the unending call of duty that the Party demands of them; their T-shirts becoming thin and tatty as the months pass after an election, only to be replaced by new ones as another election approaches. But still they seem to be making more progress than he is. At times he misses their comforting presence, especially his friend Jabu, and an overwhelming desire to go and re-join the group floods over him.

Yet how can he return when his prophet told him that it was the way of the evil one, the devil incarnate troubling the country, coming short of calling the Old Man the devil himself. This is what multiplies Maki's confusion. How can one person be Christ-like and devil-like at the same time?

***

'Behold, I present to you your surprise, the real miracle. Sit down, relax and enjoy.' Jabu whispers in Maki's ear, pointing at a plane appearing from the clouds and landing in the distance, with two others circling above it. Maki had not seen Jabu leaving but, turning, finds him gone. He wonders what Jabu had done to get so close to the Commissar who, many believe, holds so much power. Would he have managed to reach the same heights if he had chosen to hang on? Moving his mind away from the retreating figure of his friend, he watches as the large plane taxies and stops just a few metres from where they are seated, the noise deafening his ears. The praise singers, who never stopped singing, have upped their tempo.

With so much pomp, Maki guesses it could be only one person, but his heart beats faster as he imagines that it could as well be the Old Man's coffin. However, watching the Old Man walking triumphantly down the airplane stairs, unaided, fills Maki with a new respect, feelings not dissimilar to those of the disciples on the day of the ascension: awe, fear and a deity-like reverence. He cannot believe that the Prophet almost messed up his head, encouraging him to believe there can be anything better than the Old Man; and though his knowledge of truth is currently murkier than his local sewer stream, he can be forgiven for thinking that God may have reincarnated into the Old Man.

It shocks him to think that people compared him to the Old Man. He knows the comparison is not only blasphemous but stupid, especially now that he seems to be wandering aimlessly through life. No one can match the Old Man. Everyone falls short of the glory of his power and abilities, like sinners at the feet of Christ. What is he, Maki, a mere mortal-prone youth riddled by diabetes, hunger and confusion, compared to the undying, resolute and visionary Old Man who has resurrected many times and continues to defy death, and age as if they are things he can rig and cheat like elections?

The sun has begun to set, sending long beams into the horizon. From where he is sitting, Maki is looking at the Old Man's silhouette, playing like a mannequin against the deeply orange globe, and feeling euphoric, thinking that this is just about the most spiritual feeling he's ever had. For more than three hours now, the Old Man has been speaking and standing, sometimes breaking into song and dance, but never fading. He laughs about his death, he talks about his enemies, he bemoans the rains that are not coming, he rails against sanctions, he talks again about his death and about his enemies.

It is nearly ten hours since the crowd-pushers met him. Maki, who is familiar with diabetic blackouts knows that he has to get something to eat or he will have to be carried away, probably dead. Jabu, his only hope is still away with the Commissar, probably running errands. He tries to text him only to find the signal jammed. It scares him. He can feel the crumpled two one dollar notes meant for the family's breakfast and supper items that day, but Maki knows that the thought of walking away to get something to eat while the Old Man is speaking, especially from where he is seated, is not only stupid, but indistinguishable from treason.

As another blackout hits him, this time much stronger than the previous ones, Maki tumbles to the ground. Heads briefly turn to look at him sprawled precariously close to the red carpet set out on the pavement and then turn back to the Old Man, who is again talking about his death. Nothing can be done for Maki until the Old Man has finished-speaking and left the airport.

They only come out at Night

Donna Kirstein

Geoffrey hunkers down behind the pile of rotting garbage. He watches the blood drip down to the ground, each splash of red slowly separating out into a dendritic system of cracks and crevices in the concrete. Each small rivulet of red spreading out. He knows it will wash away with the rains; the most that will remain is a faint brown smudge on the cement. His blood will join the abstract stains that cover the town. The smell of shit and urine creeps up his brown trousers. His nose wrinkles, pressing his hands tightly over his mouth, he stays crouched in the alleyway. He is safe in the shadows that fill the void between the colonial and post-colonial structures. He blames the news and those damn busybodies. Not Vicky. This wasn't her fault. Several spiders' webs stretch above his head, clinging to the spaces between the bricks. The girls in his classes never enjoyed his lectures on spiders.

The sound of angry shouting moves closer. Geoffrey freezes. Was today the day? He never thought he would fall victim to them. Lately, people had been reacting violently. In Madagascar, a vigilante mob had burnt a French tourist to death. Recently, when he'd been travelling, Geoffrey had seen an angry crowd murder a stranger over an allegedly stolen fruit. In Harare, a thief had narrowly escaped when he had been caught and locked in a room. Individually, people weren't the same but a crowd always wanted blood. Today, this crowd want his blood as it drips down the side of his face. Like waves of wind in the grass, he can hear their anger evaporate, fade and resurge while they hunt him. He breathes slowly, hoping that the heat will break. Geoffrey steadies himself against the wall and strands of web snag, clinging to his fingers. He can still get himself out of this mess, he thinks. If he can just stay hidden until their rage dissolves into the hot afternoon sun and they shuffle home to their families; then he'll be all right. Didn't they know, hadn't he told the children, that they would be safe? That they would only come out at night? The last fortnight had seen two local children taken, both at night. Albino skin was a valuable and dangerous commodity. The cloudless sky seems to be holding its breath.

Soon his legs start cramping, his damp shirt clammy against his back. He stays frozen. The shadows shift and stretch as the cobwebs glint in the low angled light. Crouched in the alley, he watches his blood slowly dry, waiting for shadows to solidify into night. His pulse drums against his skull. The chatter of the day and all the noises from the street lull him into sleep.

A rough tongue wipes against Geoffrey's face, drawn by the scent of his blood. He lands a kick against the animal's side. The stray yelps and skitters off. He stretches. A dull brown spider scuttles out from under a piece of scrap metal and waves her front legs, startling him. It's a rain spider, a female; her abdomen distended. He breathes more easily, harmless, just a nocturnal hunter. His face feels raw from where the first fist landed. Dawn is close. The teacher needs to leave before the heat builds up again. There is a thrumming in the atmosphere, a humidity that has little to do with the throbbing in his side and head. Today, there is a thickness in the air that pushes into his throat, coating his skin with sheen of sweat. The heatwave might break today. Perhaps the rains will come and wash away the dust-coated tempers of yesterday. He winces in pain as he recalls his old lessons: rain spiders are often a sign of an approaching storm.

Geoffrey stumbles out of his alleyway, almost stepping onto the sleeping shape of a beggar. He knows that it's time to leave. In the hot October sun with the abduction of two children, all it had taken was one angry shout. One man with a voice that carried above the clatter of the market, marking him.

'He's the one,' the first call had sparked a righteous anger, a crackling murmur. They should have known better. His students had been playing in the dust nearby. He tried to calm the crowd.

'No!' He had tried protesting, 'I am not the one! I'm innocent!'

But someone had swung at him, and he was left with no option other than to run.

'The act of a guilty man!' Someone pointed. The shouts had spread. He had run darting across the roads, dodging overloaded kombis. His heart pounding and the glare of the sun in his eyes, fear and his high-school athletics practice had pushed him faster as he nipped around food stalls and over the outstretched hands of the homeless and disabled. Finally, Geoffrey had ducked into an alley, then another, until he had tripped, spraining his ankle. He'd crawled into the shadows to wait out the night.

Today he was alive. He could move on. Geoffrey stumbles forwards, his hand clutching his side as he passes potholed streets and corrugated iron-covered shacks that lean into each other. He weaves through the narrow roads, his attention catching on the scraps of colour as make-shift curtains peek through the open windows of the shanty shacks in the slow light of dawn, each filled with sleeping, sticky bodies. He is not far off when he sees Vicky. Leaving for school, she wears a uniform that is two sizes too small and barely covers her knees. Her close-cropped hair and pale skin seem a patch of light against the gloom. He has been forced to abandon his students.

'Vicky,' Geoffrey calls as she nears him.

'Good morning, Mr Geoffrey,' the girl curtsies respectfully, drawing her book closer.

'You need to be careful in the mornings.'

'Yes, teacher.'

'May I walk you to the school? You should be more wary of strangers, especially since...' Geoffrey pauses, 'you know...'

'Yes, teacher,' Vicky responds, her eyes downcast. 'There are people who have been taking children,' she recites back to him.

He has drummed it in over the past two months since he started working at the school, needing them to understand why, to be aware. There was always one child who would question him further. Geoffrey had hated having to explain the recent abductions. The children were vulnerable, especially children like Vicky. He glances down at her as they walk together. The warm light at their backs outlines the kinks in her hair. Her unpigmented skin and blue eyes mean that she stands out, especially during the early morning.

'Let's go this way today,' Geoffrey hobbles down a narrow lane. The dirt path winds between the crumpled rusty shacks. He doesn't want to be seen in case the memory of yesterday's accusations is still fresh in the township. He starts smiling but his cheek cracks with pain. Vicky pads silently alongside him, her bare feet hardened against the dirt. Small movements keep snagging in his peripheral vision, strangers all on their way to work, women carrying buckets with water. The temperature already rising with the sun.

He pauses outside a derelict building. The metal door is rusted red, the windows boarded shut long ago. The school isn't far off.

'Vicky, wait' he hisses, signalling she come closer. 'I need to show you something, to tell you something.'

The girl is quiet, well behaved; she hasn't even questioned his directions as they laced their way through the township maze. And with her book clasped in her hands she comes. The sunlight has reached this side street. Daylight blooms, dust motes hovering in the air around them. His ribs hurt. His head throbs and his eye feels swollen.

'I know, it's okay.' The top button of Vicky's blouse dangles. It slowly rotates on a loose thread as she pauses. 'You aren't coming back to the school with me are you, Mr Geoffrey?'

His pulse stills. 'Why would you say something like that?'

'I saw them chase you yesterday. And you want me to know that it's not safe for me. That's what you want to tell me.' Vicky stares at the ground, her bare toe worrying the sand.

'And?' he prods, leaning back into the door. His weight pushes it open slightly, the stale cool air soothing the cuts on his face.

'You told us not to go out at night, the gangs will take us, but look it's OK. The sun has risen.'

In the distance Geoffrey can hear the noise of a cockerel. There's a hum in the air as the day begins. He can hear a gurgling baby in the shallows of the township. A stranger walks past; head down, oblivious to them. He doesn't stop and turns left at the junction. The door scrapes open behind Geoffrey and he reaches down. His ankle burns.

'I told them how you walked the others to school and how you told them to be careful and not follow strangers.' Vicky continues, 'I told them how you had been working in the other school and it had happened and you just wanted us to be safe and now you've been hurt because they think it was you, but I'll tell them that you're not the one and how you helped me and walk me to school of...'

The teacher exhales slowly as the blunt side of his machete collides with the side of her head. She sways. The loose button swings back and forth. For a moment it seems that she will carry on talking, and then as she crumples, Geoffrey bends down, his ribs aching, to catch her. He pushes his back harder into the door. It opens with a scraping like nails on his chalkboard.

Gently, he half carries, half drags Vicky's limp body into the shadows of the building. Once inside, he lays her on the floor near them. His eyes struggle to adjust to the dark. His fingers scramble for her neck and only by pressing hard (reminding himself to breath slowly) can he feel a slight, small pulse. It feels, he thinks, like a butterfly trapped in a web, a faint fluttering against his fingers. He stands, feels around in his pockets for the cellphone. He didn't lose it yesterday, he had made sure of that. He dials.

'Bring the dollars,' he grunts with pain. 'Yes, I have a delivery for you, three of them. Same price as before. Good magic.' He pauses, 'Hurry, I need to move on, perhaps even across the border. It's no longer safe here.' The pounding in his head is so loud that he almost can't hear the hitched breathing of the others as they lie trussed up on the floor behind him in the dark.

Message in a Bottle

Isabella Matambanadzo

I felt the sinews of my mind stretch. And rip. This feeling took hold of me and wouldn't let me go. It came every time I thought about my mother and the things that happened to her that year. They'd tried to hide her from me, but we had our own special way of communicating. It had always been so.

I was accustomed to coming home to a neat, empty house. My key, like a precious pendant on a leather thong around my neck, clicked easily into the lock of the side door. I reached my hand inside the security gate and pulled at the switch that let me in. Once inside, I put my exhausted book bag on the floor. It has seen better days. Achemwene, the tailor who'd come to our neighbourhood from Malawi, had patched swathes of denim into the very worn sections where the armbands rubbed against my shoulders. He had smiled a big, tooth-full grin and reassured me that it was as good as new.

I pulled off my brown lace-up shoes, together with my white ankle socks, and let the cool concrete floors soothe my tired feet. We'd had athletics at school that day. The teacher was in a foul mood, so we ended up running long-distance laps. I looked down at the grey floor, waxed to a brilliant shine with Cobra. Again, I thought about the things I would do for Mama when I was grown up and working. I'd make sure she had her dream kitchen and pantry with the floors done up in those cobalt blue talavera tiles she loved so much.

I slipped on my flip-flops and moved to change into my home clothes. My single bed pushed against the wall, was draped with a faded mint-green duvet. A teddy bear Mama had given me for my birthday rested its frayed head in the hollow of my pillow. She'd bought it from a lady who lugged sacks of second-hand toys from Mozambique. The psychiatrist had a similar bear, only new. He also had a mother, so how could he be sitting safely behind his big desk asking me how I felt?

My routine was familiar. I would wash my hands with water stored in a green plastic jug, which was easy for me to lift from under the sink without spilling. That's where we kept the drums of water, which we collected in our wheelbarrow every weekend from the community borehole; it'd been put in by an international aid agency so that we wouldn't get cholera. Our small home, though it didn't use much of it with its modest proportions, hadn't had water run through its taps for more than a decade. Now I'm fourteen, but I can't remember how water flows through taps. I've never stood under a shower of warm water or known the luxury of carelessly washing twice a day with no care for the labour involved in gathering water. Don't get me wrong, I'm not complaining. It's just that I am curious about why it is this way.

At our small wooden dining table, I would first say my grace for the food that Jesus had put on our table. I'd never met Jesus because he was busy all over the world suffering for everyone's sins. When I was small, I really wanted to meet him to say thank you for the food because that was the polite thing to do. Instead, I ate the peanut butter on brown bread Mama left in a lunch box on the table for me. I always ate my afternoon snack alone. Then carefully filled a small glass with UHT milk. Even though there were lots of cows in our country, the days of fresh milk were long gone.

The milk gurgled down into my stomach like the joyful laughter of the little brother I often imagined. All the other children at school came in twos or threes. In our family it was just me. And Mama. Then just me.

I did my homework meticulously. Maths first, because I always struggled with simultaneous equations. Then science, which I enjoyed. And finally, geography. It fascinated me, the mysterious, unseen and ultra-powerful world of tectonic plates. I imagined them moving. Maybe as slowly as a tortoise. My plan then, was to become an astronaut. I wanted to go to university and then fly to the moon. I could not wait to walk on its bouncy surface, which somehow reminded me of the sweetness of the marshmallows Ma used to buy me after she'd been paid.

We'd stopped shopping for luxuries a few years ago. We now only ate meat once a week. Other days our meals were mostly *sadza ne muriwo*, the green vegetables that have an endless life and grow in our small vegetable patch at the back of our house. Or sugar beans. Or kapenta: dried fish so small it disappears in one easy swallow.

On Sundays we had chicken. Mama would catch one from her coop. She usually nabbed a youngish rooster whose meat she said was still tender, and cooked it her way. With a thick onion and tomato sauce. On Sundays, she went all out with the cooking because she didn't go to church, though she made sure that I went.

Every Sunday morning she walked me to the gate of Our Sisters of Penance Tabernacle. It was like an outing for us. We discussed the things that had happened in the previous week and our plans for the time ahead. Often, Ma came home when I was already in bed. Had I stayed up for her, I would've realised that she'd started forfeiting her evening meal, so that we had enough milk and bread for the next day's morning tea. Our mornings went by in a rush of getting out of the house on time. Me to school and she to work. Unless we shared the bucket wash together, we seldom managed a hug. Now I wish we had dawdled. Slowed those days down. I had no clue that they would be so few.

Mama would be waiting to pick me up after the service and we'd walk home hand in hand, chatting. My Bible was a hardback with a picture on the front cover of Abraham. He was the prophet who was told to sacrifice his son; the priest said the story explained the importance of faith. Of suffering. And I liked those stories. Especially when the suffering ended and the people in the Bible were triumphant. Like when Isaac survived.

When they thought I wasn't listening, people said those like my Mama were not allowed in our country. In the beginning I wondered if it was because I didn't have a father. That's when I considered myself an illegitimate child, born out of sin. Later, I learned that it was for a different reason.

Ma never responded with Amen after I'd said grace for our Sunday lunch, which was always chicken, rice in a juicy peanut butter sauce and cabbage salad with a small spread of mayonnaise. She did not even close her eyes. I knew this because I would peep and see her looking long-ingly at our gate as if she was expecting someone, and unsure if they'd come. Unlike the neighbour's houses, ours very seldom had visitors. When people walked past our home, they looked away and scampered by as if in a hurry to get away.

Aunty Zina, who called Mama *s'thandwa sami* had a pierced nose, a high-pitched voice and smoked hand-rolled cigarettes with a wick-edly sweet smell. She was Ma's only girl friend, and our regular visitor. Apart from the very tidy chap with a clip board and ballpoint pen who every month came from the municipality offices to dutifully read the water meter for the water that never came. She arrived in her flowing *shweshwe* skirts that swished before her as she eased herself from the taxi, which had picked her up at the airport. She always arrived with delicious gifts that were of little practical use. If Mama had asked her to bring us a small solar panel, so we could have light, she came with scented candles and long-stick matches claiming they were more ro-mantic. When Aunty Zina was with us, we used two-ply toilet paper, and washed with bubble bath. Actually this didn't make much sense because we only ever had bucket baths.

During Aunty Zina's visits we went to town in taxis, not squashed in a kombi. She spoke animatedly to the flower vendors at Africa Unity Square, asking after their families and how their children were doing at school. She knew them all by name. There was Felix, who used to be a certified accountant at a big firm that closed down in 2002. His wife was now a nurse in the UK, sending money for the new house they were building in Bloomingdale. Obvious, an engineer by profession, had worked as a project manager at a construction business whose own-ers had shut down and moved to live in a gated community in Jo'burg in 2003. His wife was in Perth, in Australia, near the beach working in the Army and waiting for her immigration papers to allow her to bring him over. No-Matter had worked as a clerk in a bank that had gone bust in 2006. His wife and children had managed to get into Canada before the citizenship rules changed. His wife hadn't been able to come home for her mother's funeral and No-Matter had buried his mother-in-law with a sense of aloneness and shame. He couldn't afford the cow for the funeral feast. He'd entered the U.S. diversity visa lottery through an Internet café-based pimp, to whom he'd paid $50.00, as he didn't know it was a free lottery.

It was like that with Aunty Zina. As we walked stall to stall from Third Street to Second Street – its now Sam Nujoma Avenue – but she referred to it by its old name. Second Street. She spoke to everybody with ease and familiarity. And she bought bunches of overpriced long-stemmed roses, without haggling, leaving hefty tips in the vendors hands.'Wunderbar' she would say cradling the flowers as a mother does a new baby, and slipping into the German she'd learned in Munich. It didn't matter to her that I didn't always understand what she was saying. She spoke to me in a mish-mash of her musical click-click language, German, and very grown-up English. She did not treat me in the way other people did, as if I was too young to comprehend. I tried to teach her Shona, but the only word she was interested in was 'beloved'. She used it when she spoke to my mother. 'Mudiwa' she would say giving Mama the roses, which we placed in empty peanut butter jars.

She drank too, Aunty Zina. There were always cans of beer, whisky and bottles of red wine in her suitcase. And when she drank she said it made her feel good. That's when she liked to take all her clothes off and dance around our living room in her matching underwear. I had never seen underwear that matched before. Her panties and bra were always co-ordinated. She played Miriam Makeba's music loudly on a small battery operated beat box that she always had with her. She came from Cape Town where, she drove a drop top convertible BMW, which she had brought back with her from Germany. She said her apartment had a view of the mountain and the ocean.

Mama always smiled when Aunty Zina was around. The three of us would hold hands and dance to the music which had a lot of click-click-sounds that came from deep in the throat. I fumbled along with Miriam Makeba:

aHiyo Mama, ahiyo Mama ya,
nants'i Pata Pata
aHiyo Mama, ahiyo Mama yoh,

nants'i, Pata Pata
Saguqa sath'ahi ti
Aaah saguqa sathi nantsi...

Aunty Zina gave me one of her decadent laughs. It made me feel joyful. She said I was off key and sang like a tenor rather than an alto. Her grown up English always hit me in the right place.

She once gave me a packet of tissues that had the smell of a rose garden and I wanted to keep them around me forever. But the scent faded a few days after she left us.

The two of them slept in Mama's big double bed and drank filter coffee, which Aunty Zina had brought, from one cup. In the small kitchen they squeezed between each other, broad hips rubbing a generous bum, as one of them chopped and the other stirred the pots that sat on the two-plate gas cooker. Aunty Zina's groceries should have included tinned sardines, which lasted longer and were more cost effective, but she always brought us salmon and prawns; vacuum packed on ice. She said that sodium and preservatives, which were found in tinned foods, were bad for our health. Sometimes Aunty Zina would stand behind Mama and wrap her long arms around her stomach, resting her head on her back. Even with these most mundane of chores like cooking, together they turned life into a dance.

aHiyo Mama, ahiyo Mama ya,
nants'i Pata Pata
aHiyo Mama, ahiyo Mama yoh,
nants'i, Pata Pata
Saguqa sath'ahi ti
Aaah saguqa sathi nantsi...

Zina was not her real name. It was the name people called her by. Her passport had her full name, Ntombizine. I loved the way it made my teeth grind against each other. She travelled all over the world and always sent us letters, photos and postcards as well as boxes of dark chocolate.

Afterwards the psychiatrist gave me pills to stop Mama showing me what had happened to her that year. But the pills did not work. They only made me sleep, even during the day. Maybe if they had been the bigger ones that I saw other people get they may have had an effect.

And as she always did Mama came to my side and told me what had happened.

She was walking home from her job as a civil servant. There'd been no pay since October – that was in 2014, but every day she woke up and diligently went to work. We had a miserable Christmas that year. We couldn't go shopping for new clothes or eat chicken and rice with peanut butter sauce or ice-cream with fresh mangoes. Usually we ate until our stomachs hurt. Instead we had *sadza ne muriwo* from the little garden, which was now very dry because the rains hadn't come so we couldn't water it. We didn't feel too bad though because everyone was doing the same.

The weeks went by and still in February 2015, there was no rain. Or pay. Ma had that look in her eyes. The look of suffering. She was not the only woman who had that look. All the mothers in our street had the same expression. There was no laughter in our neighborhood.

When there was electricity we'd watch the Minister for the Treasury on the television. He always looked very cross about the pay issue. I wasn't sure why, particularly at being on TV, which was so cool. Instead he foamed at the corners of his small-pursed mouth and spit always followed his words in a shower.

Mama got off the taxi late at night because her department was working long hours on some important papers that were wanted by the boss of a big, rich organization called the MFI. Ma said they gave loans and money to countries all over the world, but I didn't think it was fair that Ma and her colleagues had to work for months without pay because there were too many ghosts in the civil service. Until then, I thought the only place to find ghosts was at the community cemetery. That's why we never hung out there at night time.

By the time she turned the corner and reached our neighborhood the lights were out. Because she didn't have her torch with her, Mama walked the journey homewards in the hardness of the dark. The dark is always at its worst just after the lights go, before we fumble for the matches to light candles or remember where we left the solar lamp. That's when the thing happened. When Mama was looking downwards, not sure of where there was a shadow in the path that would trip her up, or if the stray dogs would chase after her confusing her for a thief. The

43

only thing she saw was the ripples in the pools of water that filled the pot holes. They looked like mirrors shining intermittently all over the streets. It perplexed us to see so much water flowing when it never came through our taps. I had by now lit the candle we kept near our veranda so that she could see her way from the gate. I was not allowed to leave the house when it was dark.

It was month-end and I think Mama had many things running through her head. Perhaps her feelings for Aunty Zina. But mostly she was doing calculations. Adding up how she was going to pay the rest of my school fees because the head teacher had written her a final letter of demand. I also knew the tin where we stored our maize meal was running very low. Instead of sadza, which used more maize flour, we'd started eating a very thin porridge. I didn't understand the head teacher's logic. She was also in the civil service and knew that there had been no pay since last year, so why did she bother to write rude letters to all the mothers demanding fees that did not exist? The school bursar said it was for the audit trail. Grown-ups use big terms when they think children shouldn't understand what's going on. But we do. I thought it was just a waste of paper. But grown-ups don't like to listen to kids, even when we're right, so I didn't say anything.

Mama didn't notice the small gang of people that had formed behind her. Maybe they were walking very softly. Or maybe her usually clear mind was too confused by how we would cope. I don't know. Next thing she was on her knees in a puddle, her skirts swirling in mud and one shoe missing.

One of them kicked her to the left of the head as if he were scoring a penalty shoot out goal. The thud brought her face down in the mud. And she swallowed the rusty water in a cry for help that no one heard. Mother was strong. But the gang had taken her by surprise. That's why she had no power to fight back. They drowned her in the puddle, right there in the water of the pot hole that was very near our home. And then they pulled her underpants down to her knees. One of them reached for the quarter bottle of Krango and broke its plastic base off. He thrust the neck end up between her legs.

Inside the bottle was a message. *'Ngotchani! Ngwembe!'* It read. 'Burn in hell'.

Though there were fingerprints on the bottle that provided evidence, the police didn't open a docket. Conservative officers were reluctant to rock the boat. They said it would be a messy case that would affect their superiors.

The Psychiatrist doesn't believe me when I tell him I know what happened. He says I am prone to flights of fancy. But Mama shows me everything when I'm asleep. She does not lie. I tell the Psychiatrist that they came to her funeral. The gang of quiet-footed people. I saw the mud on their shoes. They reached their hands out at me in false sorrow for my loss and hung around for the free food. Some of them even wanted to carry my mother's wooden coffin to the graveyard, which was not far from our home. They sang the choruses of the funeral songs.

Because Mama didn't go to church she was buried by her funeral policy from a firm called 'The Comforters'. The government policy was broke. The CEO had withdrawn all the money from the bank and built himself a four-storey house with an elevator and a heated swimming pool. For some bizarre reason Ma had chosen 'The Comforters' insurance that came with a singing choir.

Jehovah anotipa
Chisepe misi yese
Nekutitungamira
Mutsembwe dza Satani

Zvotanga takasungwa
Ndizvovo tinotenda
Chisepe chenyu Baba
Ndi Jesu Kristu Tenzi

If she hadn't done that it would have been a very quiet funeral, like a white person's where no one really cries or sings.

And that is how the feeling started. For a long time, the postcards arrived from Aunty Zina, who didn't know what had happened. My mind would spin with too many voices that chit-chattered over each other. They would tell me that if the MFI had paid my mother, rather than wasting its money investigating ghosts, maybe she'd have been able to buy one of those little Japanese cars and come home safely.

Sizwe Burning

Farai Mudzingwa

1

When he started burning a pall fell over the sky as it does moments before the first raindrops begin to fall.

The air is laden with moisture and darkens. The birds are the first to settle – and then there is quiet.

The first flames licked his face and he did not flinch. It was petrol and it burnt on the surface of his shirt. The flames danced over the fabric and reached upwards towards his head. He was kneeling and still. The little boy had his playing tyre resting against the front of his legs and he just stared, mesmerized. A vacant gaze. The initial burst of flame died down. The fumes had burnt out; then his clothes caught and the petrol, which had soaked into his shirt, his hair and drenched his skin turned to flame. A secondary burst of fire bathed his face and the skin started to peel away. Retreating hastily, the boy continued to watch.

He played with matches. He would stretch an empty bread packet and one of his friends would light a match beneath it or hold a flaming stick under the stretched plastic. It would rapidly shrink and drop globules of burning goo. The skin on the man's face did not form black gooey globules.

They say he was silent as he burnt.

He sputtered.

The tyre around his torso locked his arms but still he didn't struggle. They say he wouldn't have done so.

When the fire started to burn in earnest, a thick black smoke obscured him. They turned their heads and leaned in to see better. The smoke grew thicker, the stench stronger, but some got bored and walked away.

The little boy stood around for a bit longer. Even he was slightly bored. After the man had started burning, not much had happened by way of excitement. He hadn't put up a struggle – well, not after the seventh bullet – and a potentially exciting event had turned into a rather dull affair.

The flames peeled away from the skin, revealing raw pink flesh and creamy white bone. The boy's eyes widened. The smoke from the tyre quickly covered the raw face and the sooty deposits painted it black in slow brush strokes. The boy lost interest and walked away to find his friends.

2

It wasn't a secret who'd killed him; lynched him to be exact. Old Willie Lynch would have been proud of the tyre customization. They were known as Amawele – The Twins. Because they were. Not that one could tell by looking at them. True, they had the same odd bent of nose and turn of lip, to signal fraternity, or at least, a kinship of sorts. But they were different enough in stature to loosen the idea. A lazy observer would say partners or friends, perhaps even brothers, but not twins.

The short fellow was Andile and as the story goes, was the smarter of the two. Popped into the world first and then promptly began hostage negotiations for release of his brother on terms favourable to him. True, he had the brains, but he was no wimp. Even without the pistol on his hip he could whip fellows much bigger than himself into compliance – sometimes two or three at a go.

He also had that evil streak which tends to manifest itself in dimunitive men like the kids who torture insects, read books and don't go out to play. He put the first bullet through Sizwe's shoulder. The right shoulder of course. Careful to miss any arteries; opposite side from the heart; nowhere near the lung; a clean sadistic shot.

The rounds in his piece were modified. He hated death. It got in the way of pain. And so the calibre was slightly smaller than standard – and his shots measured and clinical.

The petrol and the tyre were his idea.

The other one wasn't a big fellow by international standards. Xolani. He was just bigger than his brother. And so it wasn't another case of a smaller cleverer older fellow leading a bigger, less intelligent, benign giant. No sir.

This was no silent sidekick. Xolani had been against the idea of shooting Sizwe before burning him. He reasoned that if they shot him first, then they would risk either killing him outright or having him pass out in shock; in either case, he wouldn't feel the right amount of pain.

Andile wanted Sizwe immobilized by a few well-placed shots and then burnt, in orderly fashion. Without hassle. And so after Andile had taken the first shot, which went clean through the shoulder, and seemed to deviate from the pain plan, Xolani decided to do the shooting himself and he carefully slid the next few bullets into Sizwe's arms and legs.

The little boy had appeared, popped up, after hearing the first two gunshots. A distinctive sound. He'd stood fixated, and when Xolani pumped in his fifth shot, and paused, satisfied with his handiwork, the kid's face fell. The boy frowned when Xolani placed the firearm back in its holster. Then noticing this disgruntled member of the audience, he lazily pulled the gun out again and slotted a slug into Sizwe's left shoulder. It was Xolani who dropped the tyre over Sizwe and poured the petrol over him, making sure he did not spill nor splash any on his brown Carvelas.

3

Sizwe's sister loved him with precisely that mix of devotion and spite- which only an older sister can have for her little brother. She sat in the church. A small colonial building. The Sisters and Fathers who had founded it had died long ago and it had stood vacant and disused after the last of the faith had left.

The girl was alone.

It had come to her that she should have a service or at least bring the remains of his body to the church. Their mother used to attend the services when the pastors were still around. She'd gotten her daughters baptized with the Holy Spirit and remained a member of the church until its doors shut. Then she had died. Now, Sizwe's sister had returned: her brother's charred remains encased in a casket because she knew that this is what their mother would have wanted for her little boy.

The casket lay sealed in front of the altar. The young man had spoken a few words and read some random scripture about death being the beginning of eternal life; it was then that she started to feel the loss. The casket was cheap but the brackets were clamped tight and made a strong seal – he was never coming out of there again. She wanted there to be one loose clamp; some way for him to free himself just in case he woke up. She felt her chest tighten as she pictured him waking up in the cramped darkness of the casket and feeling his way round the inside looking for a latch, trying to push the lid open. And then there were the bandages. They had insisted on cremation because the body had been so badly burnt. There was definitely no possibility of viewing before the burial.

She had paid the two attendants and they had bandaged her brother's charred corpse and let her pass by the abandoned church for a few minutes before heading for the cemetery. The bandages choked her when she imagined how tight they were around her brother's neck.

She thanked the rented preacher then signalled to the two attendants that she was done. They wheeled the casket back out of the church and into their van, and drove slowly with her to the cemetery.

The grave-diggers were drunk. They helped lower the casket and twice it almost fell sideways into the grave. The finality of death descended on her as the coffin hit the bottom of the hole. The diggers wedged in metal sheets from flattened steel drums to cover the casket and then poured wet concrete over the top.

He was never getting out now.

She felt every shovelful of dirt on her heart. A weight seemed to be pulling it down into the depths of her being. It grew heavier with each shovelful of earth. It was done. She looked at the mound, her little brother buried deep in a hole.

4

When Lerato was eight or nine years old, she and her friends had what they liked to call The Secret Club. It might have been inspired by Enid Blyton's 'The Secret Seven' but it wasn't. Only the Group A schools had Enid Blyton in their libraries. Only the Group A schools had libraries. Her classroom had a bookshelf, which, at times, held a few tattered textbooks. The Secret Club met in the veld behind Lerato's row of houses. The land was distinctive in that tall grass associated with the plains grew there – savannah grass. The rest of the township only had flat grass, a bundle and a tuft here and there.

The girls would walk home from school, change quickly out of their uniforms and then gather and file down the path behind the houses and into the tall grass. You could just about make out a few bobbing heads but mostly you couldn't see them.

One afternoon the boys decided to raid The Secret Club. It was never going to be a secret for long. And the boys grew bored in the long afternoons and needed excitement. It was a military operation complete with war cries and cow-horn formations, fire and pillaging.

But when the grass caught fire they all scattered. It blazed and spread and in just a few minutes both the boys and the girls were standing at the end of the row of houses watching the fire in awe. Then Lerato realized that Sizwe was not among them. It took only one sweeping glance before she bolted back towards their hideout disppearing into the smoke and flames. The other kids stood and stared.

Lerato sprinted down the winding footpath. Smoke blinded her. She didn't need to see: she knew her way. Reaching the spot where The Secret Club met, she saw his small form, standing, frozen, outlined against the flames, but partially obscured by the smoke.

Adults had gathered when she emerged, Sizwe slumped on her back.

5

On Wednesday morning Sizwe walked down Entabeni Street humming to himself. The kids playing in the road moved out of his way and avoided catching him in the eye. They knew him well. It is a busy street and it was doubly so that morning. A woman and her husband walked straight towards him from the taxi rank. They did not give way as they passed Sizwe, and the woman bumped Sizwe's shoulder. He turned around, pulled out a flick knife and stabbed her rapidly in the back, neck and shoulders, before her husband came between them. She collapsed on the ground and Sizwe trampled her while he stabbed her husband in the neck, chest, face and arms.

He left them in the dust and heat where they bled to death quickly while he walked away cursing himself for having dirtied his knife with blood.

A bit further down the street, a group of taxi drivers and taxi rank lay-abouts saw what had just happened and surrounded him noisily. He slit the throat of the first man to touch him and the blood shot out, squirting and spraying the close circle; they all ran away. He walked home.

The police at Unit 4 Outpost were told about the stabbings and given Sizwe's address but no one went to arrest him. He killed seven people over the next three days until his sister withdrew the R745.00 in her bank account and paid Amawele her engagement deposit.

Tsikamutanda

Naishe Nyamubaya

*T*he heat was unbearable, but life went on in the capital. The streets bustled with activity; people marching robotically like ants, hawkers yelling, cars moving. I was seated on the steps of the post-office, waiting patiently for my old friend, with my fellow, similarly disgruntled, Zimbabweans. I had just completed my A-levels and had no idea what I would become in this country. By the corner sat an old lady selling newspapers. I looked at a woman sitting two steps below me and caught sight of one of the Sunday Mail headlines which read: DROUGHT INEVITABLE IN ISOLATED VILLAGES; but as always, the H-metro headlines grabbed attention: WOMAN EATS BABY, FALSE PASTOR EXPOSED and today's read CHIEF STILL MISSING. I laughed to myself, turning my attention to a man seated below me reading The Herald. One of the headlines ran POLICE OFFICER SURVIVES BRIDGE ACCIDENT.

'Look at this, mukoma? Government should fix these roads and bridges instead of gobbling our money!' As I expected, his claim was echoed by several others, each introducing their own new grievance about the country's problems. No water, no electricity, no jobs. I laughed, then if my calculations were correct, it was the turn of the gentleman who sat beside me to add his voice to the Monday morning music. But he sat silently, reading the H-metro. 'What did that chief do this time? Juju? Snakes? Haha!' I laughed again, but the man simply turned to me with a gen-

tle smile, closing the paper. 'You shouldn't believe everything that's in the papers. But you should listen. Each one of them tells the same story.' The confidence in his eyes intrigued me and I turned to him as if I was listening, while inwardly mocking him. 'If you have time, I can join the dots for you.' I nodded, pulling an earpiece out of each ear.

The road was bumpy, but that was the case with all roads in these areas. Dylan had come to the village the year before when he'd been called by the locals to get rid of Mbuya Gova. Now, two children had gone missing without a trace and he and his new partner had been called out again. Sharlene had fallen asleep nestled in the passenger seat, her head resting against the window but jerking sideways occasionally when the car hit a bump. The quarrel he'd had with her just a few nights before still rankled, maybe he did drink too much. It was late, cold, and thick dark clouds had covered the pale white moon. With only one headlight functioning and a dozen police tickets shoved into the busted glove box, the small brown Mazda pushed its way into the darkness. They finally stopped at a small wire gate, their arrival triggering a wild response from the skinny dog chained to the gate-post. Dim candle-light appeared in the window of the first hut and an old man crawled out gripping his lantern tightly and began struggling with the gate. Sharlene woke up, rattled by the guard dog, wrinkling her face in annoyance, 'Where are we?' She sounded exhausted as she rubbed her eyes.

The gate creaked open and Dylan drove in. Following the old man's directions, he parked the car underneath a dry mango tree. 'We're here.' The dog had stopped barking and was whimpering as the old man led the way into the hut. *'Ini ndoitwa Josphat, sabhuku vatiudza kuti murikuuya'* I am Josphat, our headman told me you were coming.' Dylan smelt the damp blankets that had been laid on the floor for him and his partner; he guessed that they never expected her to be a woman. Not in this line of work. Josphat placed the lamp on the table and began heaping cold sadza and veggies onto two rusty metal plates. Sharlene had a female instinct to a stranger's food, avoid it, but Dylan whispered, 'Don't refuse it. It's rude... besides, you never know who's the bad guy.' Josphat stared at them, and Dylan felt sorry that Josphat knew they didn't want the food. *'Maita basa,* thank you.'

Josphat left, closing the door behind him. The thin flame of the lantern flickered casting shadows on the rough mud walls, the collapsing cabinets and old pictures of relatives stuck to the walls. Before long, Sharlene had sunk into the musty blankets, her sadza untouched. She had wanted them to arrive late, without all the villagers watching and staring. Regardless of the single headlight, the night-time dangers, the strange old man, the barking dog and the cold sadza, Dylan had humbly obliged, as his way of apologising for the previous night's drunkeness.

***

'Lets go,' Sharlene stood by the doorway of the hut, clad in faded blue jeans and a black T-shirt, her hair tied behind her head. Dylan tied his shoelace, seated on the folded blankets. He looked at the crinkled photograph he'd been given of the two missing little boys, before grabbing his brown leather jacket and following Charlene outside. The morning sun lay hidden in the clouds, casting a grey shadow on the surroundings. The village consisted of several shabby huts rooted in the muddy ground.

The two of them walked through the village, treading the red mud. Streams of smoke snaked into the sky from the huts. 'Its a bit strange for everyone to be cooking inside, don't you think?' Sharlene said, her voice a question mark.

Not a child was to be seen, no one was wandering around; the fields surrounding the village were dry and deserted. Two black chickens pecked the mud and an old bearded lady stared at them from her house. They stopped, and Dylan scratched his bald head, keeping his eyes focused on the surroundings. 'Hmmm. Did you speak to Josphat?'

'Yes. He said the *sabhuku* left four days ago to get help. The attacks started three days ago, people were being beaten, huts vandalised, animals are found dead, crops are dying, then two days ago, two children went missing. He said they were orphans, and the village collectively took care of them... So maybe their disappearance is related to what's been happening. They lived over there.' She gestured towards a structure ahead. A burnt hut at the end of the village, its roof gone: a blanket of black ash covered the floor, encircled by the hut's brick frame.

Dylan remembered how a cold chill had run through his body when boys at his school had threatened to beat him, and on another occasion, when his father wanted to murder his mother. He had been born with a gift, an unlikely gift, the ability to sense evil. He had put it to good use to earn a living all these years, travelling the country, ridding it of its monsters. He had built up a reputation as a highly sought after bounty hunter and, utilising a hidden identity, he had become a self-made detective of the supernatural. The locals called him *Tsikamutanda*. The ridder of evil. In Zimbabwe business was thriving. He had met Sharlene several months earlier: a beautiful, young, jobless accountant who lived next door. She had accidentally discovered Dylan's business and promised to keep it quiet if he allowed her to tail along on his missions. He enjoyed her company, and she loved the challenge of solving problems that lay out of an ordinary person's comfort zone.

Now, as Dylan stepped into the decimated hut, he felt it, a cold wave, rushing through him. 'Was this the first house to be attacked?' Dylan asked, crouching down and sifting through the ashes.

'Yes... This was where the children lived. Josphat said the attacks would stop when it rained.

'Do you feel something?' Sharlene had turned her back to him and was staring at some of the villagers who had stepped outside their homes and were murmuring amongst themselves pointing towards the hut.

'There was evil here,' Dylan said, scrutinising the remains of the burnt hut.

'Looks like the locals don't like us... Did you find something?'

Dylan pointed down at what looked like the footprint of a baby, gently pressed into the ash. He ran his little finger inside it. Then, as he raised his head, he saw what seemed to be hundreds of tiny black footprints carpeted all over the remaining mud walls of the hut. 'It's not the locals you should be worried about. I know what happened here.'

'Well?' Sharlene turned to look at him.

'It seems we may be dealing with goblins,' Dylan, looked up at her.

'What? *zvidhoma!?* Goblins? You can't be serious.'

'Well, that would explain the little feet and why no one was attacked when it rained, goblins hate water.'

'So where did they come from?' Sharlene looked bewildered.

'*Zvidhoma zvinotumwa nemunhu,* goblins have to be sent by some-one. Someone with a grudge.'

'But Josphat said almost everyone was attacked.'

'Well, that means it's someone who hates everyone, and these children the most.'

The villagers hadn't moved, neither had the sun appeared from behind the clouds. Dylan and Sharlene began walking back towards the villagers. They had instructed Josphat to gather the adults and several men and women had planted themselves on wooden benches under a dried musasa tree. Dylan stopped. 'Look, go to the meeting, find out more about the attacks, and anyone who could have had something against the children and the villagers.'

'What about you D?'

'Josphat and I are going to see the *chief kutownship.*'

'Wa... wait. No. You are leaving me here? With them? Alone?'

'Yes. Improve your people skills. Call me if you get anything.'

Dylan had already stepped into the small Mazda, with Josphat tucked beside him, wrapped in a dull misshapen jersey. As he drove out, Dylan felt a sudden guilt stir within him for leaving her, but time was of the essence, and if no leads were found soon, the children could be lost for good. The bumps on the road and Josphat's damp stench irritated him, but he held his nerve until they reached the township. It was covered in dust, bustling with people. Loud radios screamed from the few derelict shops mushroomed by vendors and hawkers. No newspapers reached this area, but Dylan wondered if the *sabhuku* had gone that far, or even taken the story to *H-metro.* Josphat pointed towards a man seated outside a beerhall between four other older men. Josphat stepped out saluting some of the bystanders who probably knew him. Dylan waited in the car, rubbing his forehead and thinking about Sharlene.

Josphat returned with the man. A faded blue cap seemed too tight on his dark, wrinkled head, and his prickly black beard looked dirty. Dylan watched as Josphat graciously allowed the stranger to sit on the front seat. 'My name is Sabhuku Chitombo,' his English was surprisingly fluent.

'Thomas.' Dylan responded with his fake name, as they firmly shook hands.

'Have you found the children?'

'No. But we will...'

'And what about the attacks?' Dylan could see the concern in his eyes.

'*Changamire, Chief,* we have reason to believe that ...*zvidhoma zvarova musha wenyu,* goblins raided your village, and most probably took the children.'

'*Zvidhoma?* No... How, can this be?'

'It's true. You left before the attacks began?'

'Yes. But I... did not know anything about...' Chitombo avoided Dylan's eyes, as if he was hiding something.

'So you, the chief, just happened to leave your village the day before the attacks occurred, and you want to return now?' Dylan clasped Chitombo's arm.

'Ah!' Josphat lunged foward from the backseat infuriated, but Chitombo raised a hand, forcing Josphat to lower the small gun that he had pulled out.

'I hope you have a license for that, *Changamire.* That is unless you have a reason for carrying it around.' Dylan let go of Chitombo's arm.

'Josphat is my brother, my security. I don't trust anyone else. But, I'm telling you the truth. I don't know anything. I left to attend a funeral and returned yesterday. You cannot accuse me of endangering my own people! I called you here. To help my people.' His eyes had reddened, but his raised voice was drowned by the radio outside.

'I apologise Sir... and what about your family?' Dylan eyed Josphat carefully.

'My wife and children left a long time ago, I live alone, with Josphat.'

The loud ringtone on Dylan's phone broke the tension in the small Mazda. It was Sharlene, her sweet voice crackled through the receiver, she should have bought an Econet line.

'Excuse me. Hullo, Sharlene?'

'*Hey D. The burnt hut belonged to a woman, her name was Constance Chidema... she left a year ago, and the children moved in. The children went missing; then the other villagers were attacked. Everyone was running scared... so they burned Constance's hut because they thought it was cursed. And it all ended.*'

'No. It's not over.'

'*What?*'

'The goblins came back even after the hut was burnt down. That would explain the black footprints on the wall, Sharley. They stepped on the ashes. They came back for something...' The phone disconnected. Dylan started the car and backed out of the township, without consulting his passengers who were silent, perhaps startled by how casual the conversation had been, considering its subject.

Later that day, they spent two hours sifting through the ashes of the burnt hut. A hot-headed reporter from *H-metro* wearing very gaudy make-up, a glossy blonde weave sewn to her head, had arrived in a white press van and taken pictures and statements from the people. Her bright pink suit clung so tightly to her corpulent body that it looked as if it could burst. Her name was Glorious. Dylan knew her, because she seemed to tail him on all his cases. He wondered how she did it, she and Boris, her fat greasy assistant, who drove her around. The feud between them was interminable due to the exaggerated articles Glorious wrote without ever seeing anything. Dylan found their wildly imaginative descriptions amusing but Sharlene and Glorious never spoke.

Two policemen had also arrived in a shiny green Defender three days late. '*Ana tsikamutanda, ndovanokonzeresa zvese izvi.* These bounty hunters are the ones who cause everything.' The constable spoke with a rasping rural accent whilst his superior silently took notes about the missing children. 'You create the problem, then we pay you to fix it. Maybe these kids ran off to the city. Hahahaha!' The laughter, sudden like vomit, was uncalled for, and the superior cast a stern eye on his constable.

'The missing children were Constance Chidema's. She left them here,' said the superior, reading off his notes. He was short and skinny and his uniform swallowed him, unlike that of the constable. The constable's name was Gurupira, he had broad features and a wooden face. By now the villagers were in their third meeting of the day. Dylan knew that the meeting with the reporters had yielded little because Glorious spoke too much concocted English, and her Shona was incredibly horrible, so he sat behind a hut listening in on the police who delved into the more logical aspects of the issue. The parents of the children? Where the children spent most of their time? Their school? Any suspected culprits? Anyone with a grudge? Any strange new faces lately? If they were Chidema's children, then the owner of the goblins had a grudge against Chidema. But who was it? Just as Dylan stood up to leave, he paused hearing an old woman saying, 'VaChidema protects the gate.' Another Chidema? He moved round the hut to see who was being referred to: things were becoming clearer.

When the meeting ended and the villagers lingered under the tree while the police were preparing to leave in their Defender to question staff at the nearby school, Dylan followed the man to his hut a distance away and stood by the crumbling brick doorway... 'Josphat Chidema.' Josphat turned sharply towards him, and Dylan felt the fear in the man's eyes, his hands twitching as if to grab something. 'Was she your wife?' Josphat shook his head, his eyes focused on Dylan. 'She was your sister, and when she left a year ago, you took care of her children. Now they're missing Josphat, and I'm guessing the reason for that gun of yours is not because you are the chief's bodyguard.' Josphat hesitated and began to sweat, as he lowered himself slowly into his old armchair. Dylan stepped inside closing the door behind him and at once the dampness of everything filled the room.

'She passed away a week ago. They said she was ill... but I know it was those *things* that did it.' He began to cry.

'Then they took the children. In the night. It's my fault. I failed to protect them. Lord forgive me.' Dylan rested a hand on the old man's shoulder.

'I can find them Josphat, before its too late. I can find them. But you have to tell me everything. Okay?' Dylan sat on the stained coffee table opposite the old man and looked at the portrait on the wall which showed a tall beautiful woman with a thick Afro, dressed in white, sitting on a *bonde* with two smartly dressed little boys standing beside her. 'Is that Constance and the children?' Josphat nodded slowly struggling to control his tears. He seemed to be murmuring something under his breath, and his fingers continued to twitch. 'Who could have done this to her?' Dylan asked intently. Josphat pulled out an old folded exercise book, and took out a black and white wedding portrait. It was the chief's wedding. Josphat was the best man with Constance as the bridesmaid.

'I had another sister, Mavis. She married the chief, that's how I became his brother-in-law. But... the chief was having an affair with Constance because Mavis could not bear children. When Mavis found out
she left. Those two children are the chief's children...'

'And where is Mavis? Where is she Josphat?'

'I don't know. No one knows. It's been years since we last saw her.'

'I bet her husband knows. Give me that gun, get Sharlene, and wait
by the car.' Dylan raised his hand. Josphat handed him the cold pistol,
which only had three rounds in it, and left, closing the door behind him.
Mavis looked even more beautiful and taller than Constance, dressed in
an old-fashioned wedding dress. The black and white photograph scared
him and he slipped it back into the exercise book. As Dylan stood up,
an eerie feeling rolled over him as he put his hand on the door to open
it. He pushed again, and again, it would not budge. He began banging
on it hard, and shouting. Josphat had locked him in, and Sharlene had
no idea where he was. He finally took a step back and kicked the door
open, shattering a part of the crumbling wall, and signalling everyone's
attention. 'Sharlene! Josphat!' The anxiety burned in his chest.

Sharlene appeared from behind a group of young men. 'What's
wrong?' A rush of relief filled him. At once he knew he really did care
for her, despite his constant denial of it.

'Where's Josphat?!'

'He left with your car, he told us you'd sent him into town.'

'Damn! He's up to something', Dylan glanced over the worried faces
of the villagers, before finally settling eyes on the white news van parked
under a tree with Boris snoring inside. 'Come on!' Sharlene had already
slid open the side door and a tired pale Glorious crawled out.

'Well, well, so now you're thieves, hm? Sharlene?' Glorious's look of
disgust was emphasised by her melting mascara.

'There's no time for bickering, Glorious, get in the van!' interrupted
Dylan, quickly easing the escalating tension between them. He hopped
in the passenger seat just as Boris was jerking himself awake and starting the van. 'Drive drive drive!' Boris moved the vehicle, his belly uncomfortably close to the steering wheel. The bumps on the road felt
worse in the van, which probably no longer had shock absorbers after
trailing Dylan and Sharlene across the country. 'Was this your plan, to

have her sitting back here with me?'

'Oh shut up Glorious,' Sharlene said in a tone of satisfaction. It was getting dark, and the sky was grey. They found Dylan's car parked beside the same bottle store they'd visited earlier. 'He's in there. Boris come with me, I'll need your help. You two stay put.' The van pulled to a stop. Dylan ran into the beerhall. He had a gift for grabbing attention, even the loud music seemed to stop. Josphat sat on a low bench resting against the wall. Boris's approach forced the men around him to clear a path.

'Where's the chief, Josphat? Did you tip him off? Come on, you're going to show us where he went.' Dylan moved aside and Boris yanked the poor old man from the seat. As they left the beerhall, alcohol-craved eyes pinned on them, Dylan was surprised to see Constable Gurupira standing by the van. Glorious had opened the side door and was asking him questions.

'What are you doing?' Dylan asked.

'What are you doing?' Gurupira turned towards them his eyes sharp and inquisitive. Everyone stared at Dylan.

'*Chef,* please, we don't want trouble, just let's finish up,' Sharlene's sudden intervention startled Glorious.

'Eh, and when you are abusing our citizens?' Gurupira said, pointing at Boris who slowly released Josphat's arm.

'Please, Officer. We'll soon be out of your hair.' Sharlene was persistent.

Minutes later, Gurupira had climbed into the white van, and the six of them were rumbling down a thin dirt road, following Josphat's directions. Boris switched on the headlights, lighting up a narrow stone bridge with a rusty yellow sign post written: NYAMATSANGA RIVER. Dylan felt the cold wind of the wide river against his cheek. 'I was afraid you'd arrest him... So I took your car and told him to run... I'm sorry.' Josphat lowered his head, sitting on the floor of the van with Gurupira and the the two women.

'Arresting the chief?' Gurupira sounded concerned.

'Now that's a killer headline, hey Boris, CHIEF ARRESTED FOR GOBLINS.' Glorious's hands choreographed the punch line.

'Shut up, Glorious,' Sharlene sounded annoyed.

'You don't have the authority to arrest anyone.' Gurupira pointed at Dylan.

'I should've listened, and not taken your car.' Josphat said sadly.

'We don't have any space in here to carry anyone else.' Boris belched.

'Where are we going anyway?'

'Shut up Glorious.' Sharlene sounded rude.

'And where's the evidence against the chief?' Gurupira poked Dylan.

'Don't tell me what to and what not to say Sharlene.' Glorious snapped.

'Hey! Everyone just calm down. Please!' Dylan said, and silence filled the van as it stopped in the middle of a clearing. A distance away stood a compound consisting of a two-roomed brick house with a corrugated iron roof, a lonely hut beside it. Even as it was getting dark, one could still see that the entire area surrounding the house had been burnt.

'Stay here,' Dylan said, but the van door had already slid open, with a worried Gurupira and eager Glorious stepping outside.

'Josphat, Officer, come with me, Sharlene, watch Glorious.' Dylan was amazed that his voice commanded order. They walked down into the centre of the compound, the door to the small house was open and a dim candle flickered through a large glass window. Dylan stopped at a distance, he could clearly hear the chief's voice and someone else's inside... '*Ndinozviziva zvawaiita naSisi vangu!*' I know what you were doing with my sister!'

'Mavis *prizi*, please.'

'*Haiwa!* Peter!' Dylan stepped inside and saw the chief sitting on a low sunken sofa, a dark thin woman wearing a black blouse and a black *duku* sat on the chair beside him facing Dylan.

'*Uyu ndiyani ko*!?' A dark anger tightened the woman's wrinkled face, stiffening her cheeks.

'Please, you must leave here.' The chief said, slightly rising from the rotting sofa.

Suddenly it all made sense: a scorned barren woman with an unfaithful husband and a backstabbing sister. The villagers must have laughed at her when her husband had cast her into the wilderness. She had sent the creatures to attack the villagers, take her husband's illegitimate children, and probably kill her sister. She bore the grudge.

'I just want the children, Chief.' Dylan held the pistol tightly in his right hand. Josphat stood by the entrance, clutching his hat, and Dylan felt the familiar cold rush flow through his body, and paced his eyes around the house in the dim light to try and discover where the evil lay.

'Please, she won't reason with anyone, she's blind.' The chief exclaimed.

'*Eh! Muaya kundipomera zvese manje*, you have come to blame everything on me now!' The woman's dark grey eyes glared at Dylan.

'The children, Chief!' Dylan cast an eye on a large brown clay pot that rested on the shelf above the woman.

'I took them in the night. I... I thought if I gave them to her she would stop. They're in the hut... outside. Please, you must not tell anyone... what I did.' The chief began to sob, lowering his head with shame.'

'Check in there, now.' Dylan pointed towards the hut outside, and Josphat and Gurupira began unbinding the wires on the door.

'*Manje hamunditore! Handiende! Hamunditore vana vangu varipo!*' you will never take me! I won't go! Not if my children are here!'

The pot began to shake and a loud piercing shriek filled the room. Dylan turned towards Josphat and Gurupira and was relieved to see the two little children clinging desperately onto their uncle Josphat, looking traumatised.

'Josphat, get into the van now!' Dylan pointed the small pistol at the woman.

Suddenly, the small house began to shake, as if it had been hit by an earthquake. Rumbling, shattered the windows, and grey dust fell from the rattling roof, the brick walls seemed to swerve around in a violent circular motion. The clay pot began to hover into the air. Mavis gave an evil cackling laugh almost falling over her chair. Pots and plates fell out of the cabinets, crashing onto the floor. A pole falling from the roof struck Dylan's hand, forcing him to drop the gun. The chief fell to the floor covering his head, whimpering at his wife's feet. Dylan struggled to stay upright, grabbing a coat hook on the wall as the house shook as if it would fall apart. Then it stopped. The house stopped shaking, the candle went out, and everything fell silent. The clay pot remained suspended in the air. Mavis sat motionless grasping the arms of her chair, slowly exposing a devious toothy grin. Then the clay pot exploded with so much force that Dylan was thrown out of the house, falling onto his back on the dusty ground. Stunned but gazing back through the broken window, he could see that thick black smoke filled the house, belching out of the door and the window and cracks in the roof.

In the midst of the smoke, a small, bald, naked creature with bright yellow eyes stood in the doorway, facing Dylan. Its skin as black as tar, its small hands and feet elongated by long sharp claws; it was no larger than a three-year-old. He knew what it was. A Goblin.

Gurupira, Josphat and Sharlene, stood outside the van whilst Glorious took pictures of the children and the surrounding area. Dylan stood up and ran shakily toward's them.

'There he is.' Glorious pointed her camera towards him, while Gurupira held his sjambok and handcuffs at the ready.

'Get in the van! Get in the van!' Dylan shouted, waving his hands wildly. Gurupira lowered his sjambok, his face empty of expression. Glorious dropped the camera as an army of black monsters charged after Dylan, shrieking wildly, their feet thundering, like a black wave flowing out of the compound. Josphat threw himself and the children into the van, and Sharlene grabbed Glorious by her weave pulling her in as she screamed. Gurupira stood as still as a wooden post. Dylan knocked the large man out of his trance, and the two of them hurriedly clambered into the van.

'Close the door!'

Josphat slid the door shut, slicing off one of the creature's thin black arms in the process. Glorious screamed. The creatures circled them and began to climb all over the van, rocking it from side to side. Gurupira lay on the floor petrified, while Josphat held the children in his arms.

'Boris!' Dylan looked at Sharlene who was trying to remain calm.

'I'm trying! It won't start! What the hell are those things?' Boris turned the key but the van's engine was struggling. The creatures began to beat at the windows, scratching them violently and large cracks sprouted across the windscreen. The small white van was smothered by the black creatures, rocking to and fro, and side to side.

'There must be a hundred of them D. We can't win.' Sharlene held Glorious tightly in her arms, whether she was muffling her cries or comforting her, Dylan didn't know but what he did know, was that if the goblins got in, they would rip everyone apart. The front wheels were punctured, releasing a wheezing sound as the van dropped to its rims. A goblin had forced its hand through the windscreen and lunged at Boris's face. Dylan watched in horror, and time seemed to stand still. The little children had closed their eyes and ears and were singing a Shona song, Josphat seemed to be praying under his breath, Glorious wouldn't stop screaming, Sharlene looked frightened for the first time, and Gurupira lay solid on the floor of the van. Suddenly the engine ignited! The lights glared and Boris punched the battered vehicle into reverse, crushing the goblins that stood behind it, whilst several others remained clinging to the roof and the bonnet.

Dylan grabbed a camera stand and jabbed it at another goblin, which was trying to enter through the floor. The van continued moving backwards into the darkness, while the headights shone on the many goblins chasing after the van. Glorious's screams drowned out the children's singing. Boris suddenly saw the bridge behind them, flattening his foot on the brakes, and forcing the van to come to a screeching halt, but it was too late. They'd veered onto the stone bridge, the rear of the van dipping down towards the river, while the front of the van was suspended in the air. Boris struggled to breathe; fine white smoke was escaping from the engine. Then, with a gasp of relief, Dylan fell back. The van rocked backwards, creeking as if it was about to fall. Dylan dropped the camera stand, and grabbed the passenger seat to pull himself up and the van rocked foward. Hundreds of yellow eyes glared at them from the other side of the bridge.

'The water! You said they hated water, that's why no one was attacked when it rained.' Sharlene let go of Glorious and moved to the back: the van jerked further backwards.

'We don't know how deep it is, we could drown!' Dylan moved to the front of the van to balance the weight, causing the van to tilt foward like a see-saw.

'We don't have a choice.' Sharlene lay back on the back panels of the van, causing it to creek and rock backwards. She was right. The yellow eyes were drawing closer.

'Everyone hang on!' Dylan closed his eyes, leaned backwards, and the van fell over the bridge.

My friend had called me seven times but I had ignored him. I was paying attention to the strange man I'd just met. It seemed to all make sense now. The headlines... He told me that the river was shallow and that they'd escaped out of the van the next morning. And, in order to avoid an even bigger investigation, they had left Gurupira stunned in the van and got away, claiming that he had commandeered the van from them earlier.

(POLICE OFFICER SURVIVES BRIDGE ACCIDENT).

He told me that Boris took sick leave, claiming to have been attacked by a dog, and was recovering in hospital. Glorious went with the story of the chief's disappearance and extra-marital activities, because the editor felt her account was too far-fetched. The only evidence of the encounter was in the camera she'd lost at the scene.

(CHIEF STILL MISSING).

He told me how the goblins had destroyed the crops in the area.

(DROUGHT INEVITABLE IN ISOLATED VILLAGES).

And that Josphat as Chitombo's next of kin was elected as the new chief, and the children were safe. He looked at me: 'Do you understand?' he asked shaking his head. Then he continued: *There was no evidence. Glorious had lost her camera, and Gurupira, had probably been admitted into a hospital for the insane.* I shook my head. Either this man was extraordinarily imaginative or he had told me an incredibly hard-to-believe true story.

'So what happened to Mavis? Is she still alive? And the goblins? And the chief?' I asked. *He rolled up his newspaper, placed it on the steps and rose to his feet. A small Mazda 323 with a young lady driving had come to a stop in front of us. The man walked down the steps, and round to the passenger door.* 'Wait. So it's not over is it?' I asked eagerly, rising to my feet. *He opened the door and paused, looking straight into my eyes.* 'No. It's only the beginning.'

The Mazda drove off disappearing into the bustling metropolis. And as I sat down on the steps, I noticed a small digital camera tucked in the rolled up newspaper the man had left behind. A tag tied to the camera read, **'GLORIOUS PRESS USE ONLY.'**

It couldn't be. Slowly, I turned it on: what would I see?

I gasped, gazing all around me, at everyone, at everything.

Agnes takes the Rap

Jo Saunders

Sergeant Tendai Choto of the Zimbabwe Republic Police sits on the bench outside the village sub-station. The afternoon sun casts short shadows across the lawn, and the breeze makes patterns in the unmown grass. Like on water, he thinks. And along comes a butterfly, white against the autumn yellows and browns. And another. Together they make other arrangements, dancing over the grass. Life is all about patterns, muses Tendai. Every which way you look at it, there's a design to be seen. *Mware*, the great weaver, Hallelujah!

At his feet lies Ninja, unconcerned by the portent of the scenery, but one eye is slightly open, and he is, as always, ready to move at an instant's notice.

Business is slack; the only juicy crime is to do with a theft of diamonds from an attaché case at the airport – there is a national alert – but diamonds could be hidden anywhere, and are probably out of the country by now, not likely to show up here. Here at his sub-station things have been relatively quiet since the mystery of the disappearing body last month – now that was an interesting case.

Ninja breaks into his reverie; the dog sits up quivering, and is suddenly gone, shooting along the track towards the road, his brindled back a blur, to intercept an approaching pedestrian, a man in jeans and a worn leather jacket. Tendai marvels. What new piece of fabric is being woven now?

Tendai notices the unfolding of events. Ninja skids to a halt beside the man who has frozen in apprehension, though without fear; this man knows dogs. Then as Ninja walks around him, sniffing at his trousers, the man relaxes and resumes his journey. Together they near the station, giving Tendai ample time to take stock. Ninja is herding the visitor towards him. The man has grey in his hair and walks like a soldier, but his face is that of a worried child.

After exchanging the greetings appropriate to the time of day, Tendai asks the man how he can be of service.

The man, his name is Joseph, explains that he lives in Harare, but has come to the village to visit his sister Agnes. Agnes works as a domestic at the big farm across the river, the one with the fishpond and statue of Adonis inside the gates. The farm was acquired by the Msawi family ten years previously. He has been to visit her, only to find a bad scene. The madam's cellphone has gone missing – and Agnes, as the only person who had been nearby, excluding the family, is suspected of theft. Agnes tells him that she is always blamed when somebody loses something. Agnes has been studying psychology by correspondence for several years and doesn't normally get too upset by these accusations. But Madam's cellphone? This is serious.

They, the Msawis, are about to use kangaroo court tactics and fire her, he said. They did not even consider calling the police, and reacted badly when he said that *he* would.

Why kangaroo court and not buffalo court, or rhinoceros justice, wonders Tendai, no kangaroos here.

The visitor, Joseph, unmindful of Tendai's musings, continues his tale. He'd told them he was a major in the army, but they were not too impressed; however they agreed not to go any further until they heard what transpired after he'd told the police.

Were both the Msawis in? No, just the wife, and her spoiled son, Freddie. The wife had mislaid the cellphone, and the wife was accusing Agnes of stealing it. Using the land-line in front of Joseph, Madam had phoned her husband, Robert Msawi, to inform him.

'What did your sister, Agnes, say about this?' Tendai asks, opening his notebook. 'She was not around,' says Joseph. 'She was in the garden picking vegetables when the loss was noted. Agnes said she never ever touched the phone as the madam would kill her if she did.'

'And when did "the madam" last use her cellphone?' Tendai disapproved, as he preferred Shona terms for Shona people. What was wrong with 'Amai'?

'She was playing Freecell in the bath at 8 a.m., the madam was, and could not remember seeing the phone again until she wanted to phone her husband at lunchtime, and couldn't find it.'

**

Freddie the ten-year-old scion has been eying his mum's cellphone for a long while. It has a new game on it, Angry Birds, and he's been itching to play it. He now sits in the avocado tree, one of several standing along the driveway, happily playing, unaware of the domino effect of his act of 'borrowing'.

He'd not been able to believe his luck ... when he'd gone to the bathroom there lay the gleaming gadget, lying invitingly on the bathroom stool, cover open, begging investigation. Freddie quickly locked the door, forbidden, but he knew he could get away with it as mum was 'putting on her face' which always took ages, and Agnes was hoovering downstairs. He lovingly fondled the phone, then cautiously pressed the 'on' switch. This was a new slimline Prestigio. And all he had was an old Nokia. His dad said the old phones were the best, but, as his mum said, his dad sometimes had odd ideas.

Freddie was trembling with excitement.

He swiped the screen a few times to get the feel of it and quickly located the game. He tapped the icon to open it up, but his heightened senses alerted him to the silence – Agnes had turned off the Hoover. She'd be coming up here soon. He quickly slipped the phone into his lower pants pocket as he'd seen bigger boys do, and quietly unlocked the door. He tried to 'act cool' as he ran downstairs, ignored Agnes who was carrying the vacuum cleaner through the hall, and he went out through the kitchen and down the glitter-stone drive to the big avocado tree near the fishpond at the edge of the property. The fishpond is his father's hobby. A former gardener had neglected it and fish had died, and now only Freddie's father, Robert Msawi, cares for the fish and the pond, and this he does obsessively: nobody else must touch the pond.

In the tree Freddie has a perch from where he can watch the fish, a lovely broad branch where he can recline, legs crossed, his back against the trunk, just high enough to avoid being seen by the casual observer. And today he wears a dark T-shirt and blotchy fatigues, his holiday uniform. Perfect camouflage if he stays still.

Out comes the phone, and he starts playing. Only a talented observer might spot young Freddie Msawi up that tree swiping away at the bright screen. And that same observer would think that Freddie is an old hand.

***

Agnes sits on her bed, dry eyed. She has been with the Msawis just over ten years; indeed, since they arrived in the village. During that time she's been accused of taking many things, but the items have always been found, having been mislaid by the family. She's not particularly worried, but knows to lie low until the tension blows over, lest she be suspected of taking other goods. Once one thing disappears suspicion becomes rife, she has observed, suddenly the Madam is rushing around, checking the levels of sugar and coffee, the stocks of soap and toilet paper in the cupboard, and her precious creams and make-up on the Dolly Varden dressing table, a period piece which 'came' with the farm, and of which the Madam is unaccountably proud. Agnes sees the piece as an embodiment of Madam's neurosis, and the frilly drapes are a nightmare when it comes to ironing; she had removed the cord the first time and it had taken ages to get them to fit later, and the large flowers never did match up in the front again, so now she has to wash and iron the fancy drapes all drawn tight on their cord which makes for hard work. She has offered to sew a new drape with tie-and-die cloth, which she makes as a hobby and which is very popular in the city markets (Madam doesn't know about this side-line), but Madam tells her she's an ignorant peasant and that her 'antique' dressing table covers would continue to be used until they fell apart.

Agnes does not think much of the Madam. Instead of going to university, the older woman had been to secretarial college, where she learned, from the racks of old publications in the common room, that The 'Rhodesian Woman and Home' taught the art of being a fine English lady. Madam had studied these aged magazines, and thought she knew it all, and she lived her life accordingly, English to the hilt (but her accent was dreadful). Everybody called her Madam, as though it was her real name. Agnes wondered if her employer ever guessed that by calling her that name they were not being kind.

'Agnes? Where are you? We need a snack – I am sure Freddie is hungry – where is Freddie?'

Agnes doesn't answer, and hears the angry clacking of Madam's heels get louder. No knock, she just barges in. 'What are you doing here girl? Sulking? This household doesn't run itself! Quickly now!'

'But you said you were going to fire me. You don't want a suspected thief working in your lovely kitchen, do you?' Agnes has trodden this path several times before.

'Well I haven't got time to prepare the food myself and get ready for the braai this evening. I must shop for the *nyama* and beer, and get vegetables so you can make coleslaw and sadza. But first some sandwiches. Freddie must be starving.' Madam is looking at the varnish on her nails – it has smudged.

'I'm sitting here until Joseph comes back. He'll tell us what the police say.'

'Oh come on girl. Work needs doing. You're not fired yet.'

'No, no work. You accused me. I am waiting here.'

'Very well. You'll regret this,' which is what Madam always says at this point.

The heels clack away down the parquet-tiled corridor, and in a while Agnes can hear Madam's voice yelling for Freddie. She last saw Freddie sneaking off into the garden several hours ago, when she was bringing the Hoover upstairs… and he was behaving oddly, furtively, bent over, hand over his lower pockets… Freddie! Freddie has the phone! Agnes is suddenly sure of this, he has often begged his mother to allow him to play games on it. What has taken her so long to realize that her son has 'borrowed' her phone? She has known Freddie all his life… her precious charge, always so open… we all grow up, learn the bad ways. But what to do now? If she accuses him, he'll lose the phone quickly to avoid punishment. Telling Madam is out of the question, she'll not hear a word against her boy. She must wait for Joseph to return. They need a plan.

***

Sergeant Tendai Choto, having left a note on the door and shut up shop, walks to the farm with Joseph. Ninja, of course, is with them, and several curious small boys join them for a while, trying to catch Ninja, who joyously stays a few steps ahead of them. The shadows are lengthening, making new patterns, but Joseph does not seem interested. Ah well, Mwari is good, and has all sorts of children. They stroll along happily, it is a lovely afternoon.

When they reach the bridge, Tendai stops. He loves the river. Fed from the hills above, with not many villages along it, it bubbles along, looking clear and inviting. More a stream than a river at this time of year, especially after the drought. There's a slight breeze, and a clean fresh smell, free of dust. He admires the reflections of the trees on the water and the way the bridge casts a shadow. Ninja rushes down for a gleeful swim, followed by several small boys, one of whom falls in after slipping on a rock. No harm; the afternoon is warm and the stream is shallow; his mates help him up. A happy crew.

Reluctantly Tendai succumbs to Joseph's request to move on, and they continue along the road to the farm. The small boys drop away, they are not made welcome by the rich family who lives there, although the son seems lonely. Ninja enjoys shaking the water off his short fur and is dry by the time they reach the gates.

***

Freddie becomes aware of his mother's voice. Simultaneously he notices how stiff he is, he has been crouched over the phone for several hours. He stretches, his cramped fingers fumble and gravity does the rest. The precious phone falls, skids off the branch, and disappears into the leaves down below. Freddie is stricken … what if the thing is broken? He scuttles down the tree – his mother is still some way away, her high heels scrunching on the rough glitter-stone, but she knows his pet places … he crouches on the ground and sweeps at the leaves with his hands. Yuck, they are all slimy and there is a rotten smell – the gardener does not rake here, and it rained yesterday. He panics – the feeling exacerbated by the sound of those heels. Where is the phone? He sweeps larger circles, hearing his mother's calls coming nearer – and getting angrier. At last his feeling fingers find the phone, now damp and scuffed with loam and muck. Thankfully he shoves it back in his pocket, mindless of the dirt, and standing, wipes his hands on his pants. He steps out into the drive to meet his mother.

'Freddie, there you are, why didn't you answer me? And why are you all dirty? Look at your hands!'

'I'm OK Ma, I fell out of the tree – I was sleeping and started falling when I heard you.'

'Oh my poor baby ...'

'I'm fine, Ma, the ground is really soft there ...' Freddie was not allowed to call his mother 'Mai' or even the more respectful 'Amai'. His mother wanted him to speak English properly. She felt that 'Mama' was best – she had read Jane Austen, and seen the movies. But his schoolfriends laughed at him: many were anti-English. So mother and son had compromised on 'Ma'.

'But you're so so dirty!' his mother shook her head. 'Come to the house, you must wash and then I'll make you a sandwich.'

'Where's Agnes? I don't like your sandwiches, you don't make them as nicely as she does.'

'Oh, the stupid girl has stolen my cellphone and we're waiting for the police. Come now.'

Freddie panics. What to do? A life of his mother's sandwich-making stretches interminably before him.

'Okay Ma, I'm going to wash!' and he streaks off back to the house, leaving her to totter along the drive in her heels.

Freddie, unmindful of the loam on his trainers, sprints through the kitchen and the hallway, up the stairs and to his parent's room. Where can he put the phone? He looks about, and sees the forbidden dressing table – only his mother may open the curtains. He charges across to it, and tweaks the curtain aside, and sees a handy low shelf with small scissors, nail-files and the little bottles of nail polish that he so coveted when he was younger. Snatching the phone from his pocket he pushes it onto the shelf, not noticing that the action causes several items fall over, so great is his panic and haste. He runs from the room and is busying himself in the bathroom by the time his mother returns.

***

Agnes hears Freddie pounding up the stairs and tearing into his mother's room. What is he up to? She can guess. A short silence, then she hears him cross the landing to the bathroom, and the sound of running water. He finishes and thumps down the stairs.

After a while Agnes stands up and crosses to the barred window of her room. Where is Joseph? He has been gone a long time. She looks along the drive, and sees two men and a dog standing by the fishpond in the circle at the end of the drive near the gates. They seem interested in the fish, one man bends down and puts his arm in the water. Boss Robert wouldn't like that. Nobody must go near his precious fish. They start walking casually towards the house. Both men have a military bearing. One, she sees, is her brother. The other is a kindly looking member of the Zimbabwe Republic Police force, neat in his blue pants and grey jersey, cloth cap back on his head. The dog, she notes, has stripes, charcoal on yellow-grey. A happy trio, enjoying an afternoon stroll. Where is their sense of urgency? Men! She returns to her seat on her bed. Her waiting is not yet over.

***

Madam and Freddie have just started eating their sandwiches when there's a ring on the doorbell.

'I'll go!' says Freddie.

'No stay, they can wait ...' says his mother but he ignores her; perhaps he didn't hear, he is halfway to the door.

He opens it, and sees the two men, one a policeman. He greets them courteously, 'Can I help you?' he asks.

Joseph, who Freddie had seen earlier, says 'This is Sergeant Choto from the ZRP. Are your parents at home?'

'My mother is. What do you want?'

'To speak with your mother, young man,' said Joseph, who looked as though he would blow flame, but smiled anyway.

'I am here, gentlemen,' says Madam from behind Freddie. Gentlemen, do come through. Freddie, finish your sandwich and go and play.'

Freddie knows when he's not wanted. And he does not want the sandwich. He runs out into the garden and squats outside the lounge window, a good position when he's excluded from conversations.

Somehow the sound of voices carries beautifully to this point. He hears the questions and the answers, where is her husband? When will he be back? This evening, good, for a braai? Fine. When did she discover the loss? What did she do? Has she actually fired the maid? Has the cellphone been found? Has the maid's room been searched? Where is the maid now? Will Mrs Msawi give permission for them to search the house? Of course.

Freddie trembles with anticipation. Soon the phone will be found and his beloved Agnes will be okay.

The adults leave the room. Freddie sits for a bit, then wanders off down the garden. There is an old mango tree he hasn't climbed for a while. Weaver birds used to nest in it. He'll go and see what he can find.

***

Madam leaves the men to it. They announce their intention of looking through the public rooms, then the bathrooms, and then all the bedrooms. Madam complies – her nail varnish is smudged and needs a repair. She thankfully escapes to her room and sits before her beloved Dolly Varden, studying her visage in the triple mirror. She pats her hair, perfect. Still a good looker, she thinks to herself. She'll stun them all at the braai this evening. All those accountants and lawyers with their ugly wives. Her husband is a financier, and has to know the right people.

Back to her nails. She reaches down – is that a streak of dirt on her precious floral drape? Just as well Agnes is going, she's getting lazy. Madam opens the curtain and reaches for her manicure file – and her hand falls on … it feels like a phone … it is a phone … it is her phone! She is so surprised that she lets out a squeal of delight, which she tries to suppress, but it is too late – the dog comes pounding in, followed by the two men, and she is caught holding the contraband …

'Uh, I … found this … on my nails' shelf …' she points down to show them where.

'May I see?' Tendai gently takes the phone from her, using his clean white handkerchief, and studies it. 'This definitely is your cellphone, the one you said Agnes stole?'

'Uh, yes… She must have returned it …'

'Or perhaps you yourself put it there in an absent-minded way after your bath. You said you came in here to do your nails?'

'Oh no, it wasn't there, I store all my varnishes there as well as my manicure set. I was taking things out and replacing them all the time I was here. The phone would have been in the way, I'd have put it some-where else.'

'Do you still want to charge Agnes?'

'Um, well... She wasted a lot of our day... She should be punished, shouldn't she, for wasting your time too.'

'Before we do that I'd like to have the phone dusted, and checked for her prints.' Tendai looks at the phone.

'But I need the phone; you'd have to take it away for that.' Madam reaches for the phone, Tendai holds it from her.

'I'd like to see the maid now,' he says, heading for the door.

Madam is not one to sulk. She finishes her nail repair and goes downstairs to check what needs doing for the braai.

***

Joseph leads Tendai to Agnes's room. After introductions, Tendai says to Agnes, 'I need to take your prints, then we'll dust the phone and check if you've touched it.'

'Welcome,' says Agnes. 'I've never touched that phone in my life. Anyway, don't thieves use gloves so as not to leave prints?'

This girl does not act guilty, thinks Tendai. And there's dirt on the phone, he has seen the trail of dirt through the house, and on the dressing table curtain, and muck on the knees of young Freddy's jeans, and on his shoes; Freddie's hands had been clean, but there had been dirt around his nails.

'I don't think we'll bother with the prints. I somehow think the prints we'll find will be those of a younger person ...'

'Oh!' said Agnes, raising her hand to her mouth, her eyes wide, 'how did you know?'

'Simple deduction,' said Tendai, 'More to the point, how did you know? And why did you not say anything to defend yourself?'

'I couldn't ...' said Agnes.

'I think I understand,' said Tendai.

'Which is more than I do,' said Joseph from the doorway, 'will somebody kindly explain?'

***

On the way out, Tendai and Ninja again stop to admire the fishpond. There are not too many fishponds, with fish, around anymore. This one has a one-metre-high statue of Adonis on a dish in the centre, his shadow is long in the afternoon light. A few rays of sun penetrate the water and a strip of the pond's glitter-stone floor still twinkles gently through the water. Goldfish dart around the water plants. Ninja watches with interest as Tendai kneels down and feels the water. He rolls up his sleeve and puts his arm in, grabbing at a large lazy fish which swims languidly away, what a pity, thinks Ninja, it may be good to eat. Ninja sees Tendai's hand scraping the bottom of the pond. Then the man stands, and wipes his arm dry on his handkerchief.

They resume their journey.

***

Madam thankfully clutches her prodigal phone. She notices that it is rather dirty – strange, that. She turns it on and it shows her a strange dark screen with cartoon birds peering out at her, she tuts, she is in a hurry as usual, these phones have minds of their own, all sorts of strange things come up. She hits escape until she finds her screensaver, a picture of a Ferrari coupe with a bescarved woman in it – herself, she believes. But that is all in her future... the braai guests will soon arrive... she hopes Agnes has finished making the coleslaw.

***

Robert Msawi arrives home that evening, irritable after a frustrating day, but looking forward to unwinding in company, with a few beers.

He shouts a greeting, then goes upstairs to wash and change.

When he comes down, smart in an open-necked shirt and casual trousers, crocodile skin moccasins peeping under their turn-ups, he goes to the veranda to check that the beers are ready behind the bar, he might even open one... but he is surprised by the appearance of a policeman.

'Robert Msawi? My name is Sergeant Choto, Zimbabwe Republic Police.'

'Ah! Is this about my wife's phone? Annoying thing, but I understand it has been found and the maid is being given another chance.'

'The maid is innocent. And no, it is not because of the phone that we are here this time.' Two other policemen step forward out of the gloom to flank him. 'Robert Msawi, we are here to arrest you on the charge of unlawfully hoarding diamonds, property of the state, in your fish-pond.'

77

Thembani's Killer

Bongani Sibanda

It was the second time since Thembani died that the police had come to question her. The first time a white detective with a freckled face and dishevelled head had arrived in a small van, acting like the humblest and most compassionate person in the world. He had asked her where she was when her husband was shot and killed in Centurion on the evening of 23 July, and continued to ask her about their relationship, even though her husband was dead: had he an affair with Agnes or was he only there to see his kid? He had insisted that she tell only the truth as any falsehood would have unhealthy implications. Indignant, she had only sobbed and let her mother and brother take the questions. The wound had still been fresh then.

Now, a week later, with the funeral and the memorial service behind her, a small man with the voice of a woman, who had identified himself as Detective Molapo and told her that Detective Cohen's health was failing which was why he was taking over, was seated in her lounge, drinking her tea, and asking her similar questions, suspicion evident in every syllable of every word he uttered. As if she could poison him, she thought. How could they?

'The thing is, Ma'am,' Detective Molapo said, playing with the handle of the teacup. 'We want to catch your husband's murderer. So that we catch the person behind it – the mastermind. See, we're very much convinced it was a hit. They only took the cellphone. But they were not really after it.'

'All I want is that my husband's killer be caught and punished,' Nolwazi said. 'That's all.'

'That's why any information you give us would be helpful. We cannot do without your co-operation.'

'And how,' she asked, beginning to feel riled, 'do you suppose I would know the person who killed my husband? He died with Agnes. Why don't you ask *her*. In any case, if I knew who'd killed my husband, wouldn't I have told you long back?'

Detective Molapo continued to drink his tea slowly and quietly as if he had forgotten where he was and what business he was about. Finished, he carefully replaced the cup on the saucer on the tea-table, coughed and rubbed his forehead; then, standing up, said: 'All I want to know is … as far as you know, what was the state of their relationship, and how would she stand to benefit should he die?'

'You're asking me if my husband was cheating on me or not? All I know is what I said in my official statement: when he left, he told me that he was going to KZN to see his parents for the weekend.'

'But did you suspect that perhaps he was cheating on you?'

'Detective!' she said, working hard to restrain herself. 'I don't know what you aim to achieve with such insensitive and intrusive questions. All I'm willing to tell you is that my husband and I had talked about *that* woman and had come to an understanding. That's all.'

They were outside on the porch when Detective Molapo looked her in the eyes and told her he was sorry for her loss.

'Be assured that we will do our best to catch both the culprit and the mastermind.'

'Then why don't you arrest that bitch? He died at her house. Who else could have intentionally left the gate open for them? No. You're not doing everything you can. You're saying you're doing everything but you're not,' she snapped. 'That's the way *she* was when *she* had the chance.'

'See,' Detective Molapo said with carefully assumed patience. 'We'll catch your husband's killer. It's our priority. But arrest Agnes without evidence we won't. She is our major suspect considering her dirty past. But arresting someone with no solid case could only foil the investigations. Let us first do the ground work.'

Nolwazi felt that she should jump at the man and bite his head off. What ground work?

'She should direct you to her thugs,' she said. 'How about that?'

'It won't work that way. But trust me, Ma'am, we're close.'

Just then, Detective Molapo's cellphone rang. He put it to his ear and listened. A minute later he was rushing to his car, telling Nolwazi that there has been some developments. He was wanted at the station.

'Trust me, Ma'am, we're going to nab your husband's killer, whatever it takes.'

For a long moment, Nolwazi remained standing at the front porch of her house, thinking.

The day rolled on same as every other day. Both her husband's daughters were at her mother's in Soweto. She was left alone in the big house. Her sister in Zone 6 had wanted to come and keep her company, but she had refused, telling her she preferred to be left alone. And so, as on all the other days, she continued with housework, cleaning the already clean house again. She had given her maid leave two weeks before her husband was killed, and the girl hadn't returned. She changed the bed sheets, the curtains, emptied the dustbin, and burned a few papers … then went to the Spar across the street to buy teabags that she already had.

Their house was directly over the road from the Spar, beyond which,- to the north, was a train station. Thembani had bought it four years ago as a birthday present for her. That was the time when the second album *Nyangazonke* came out. Those were the best of times. Their love had been strong and inviolable.

And then along came *that woman*. It was her friend who had first told her Thembani was having an affair with Agnes. Of all people – Agnes, a glamorous model with a string of angry or broken-hearted former lovers – she could not believe it. But the photos had confirmed it. And he did not deny it when she confronted him. 'A stupid mistake,' he had said; 'it will never happen again,' he told her.

Nolwazi had met Thembani while they were still teenagers, before he became this singer, attracting both houseflies and butterflies. She had been there as he rose to become the international hip-hop icon he was when he died. Despite the late nights, the drinking and the parties, never once had he given her any trouble. He wanted peace and stability as much as she did, and this had made them a strong couple.

After discovering that Agnes was pregnant when he'd terminated the affair, they had sat down and planned. There was no need to fight over it. It was just one of those downs common in all relationships, Nolwazi had told herself. Besides, he seemed very sorry. They agreed that the child would be looked after like all their children. And if he visited Agnes to see the child they would go together.

After the tragedy, Nolwazi had been given leave from work to grieve, and now all she could do with her time was read magazines and think what could life mean for her now? Yes, she would find another man, but could that man mean as much to her as Thembani had meant? Certainly not. Thembani had been a pillar in her life. She had built her life around him, under him, and on top of him. It pained her heart knowing that she wouldn't be able to give her children a true father anymore. She felt as if she was sinking into a deep hole. She forced herself to rise from the bed and stand on her feet. She could now see that her life was unofficially over, whatever she might think or do. Maybe that's the way things were meant to be. You start well, she thought, and things go bad along the way; regaining stability becomes a hope for another world.

As the day progressed, the dark rain clouds cleared and at around 4 p.m. it was hot. After taking a shower, she shut herself in their bedroom, now her bedroom, and read magazines. She couldn't remember when she had had last eaten – she was only surviving on tea, yet she never felt hungry, only a slight nausea and headache.

Evening came with no news and the night was like all the others, filled with stupid dreams. One she remembered the next morning featured a drunken motorist who wanted to run her over. The man had been laughing in the process. In the dream she knew him, but when she woke up she could not think who it was. Maybe someone wanted to frame her for Thembani's death.

Promising a bright hot spring day, Tuesday morning turned a glassy orange, and found her aimlessly roaming the courtyard of her house. She had slept little and woken up early, feeling the overpowering urge to get some fresh air. She could swear she had been chased out of her house by demons, nonsense she had once believed in, growing up in the village. Shortly before nine, her mother called for the eighth time in as many days, to ask her how she was doing, and why didn't she come over to spend some time with the children, or should she come over herself? Nolwazi declined both offers. She needed solitude, she said.

At noon, Detective Molapo called again. He was becoming a nuisance, like everything else, and she considered ignoring him. With his effeminate voice, he told her that they'd found the man who killed her husband.

What?! Not even Nolwazi could have imagined the sudden fright she felt upon hearing this news.

His name was Edmund Ngulube, Detective Moplapo said. He too was dead. And what they were doing was trying to find his killer, while also establishing the connection he had with Agnes.

'Clever woman,' Detective Molapo said, 'she got him killed to complicate the case. But we'll bust her trust me.'

'That's what I'm waiting to see, Detective,' Nolwazi responded quietly.

'We're using every means. Even if they last had a contact ten or fifteen years ago, or they had a friend of a friend of a friend as link, we'll uncover it.'

'Keep me posted.'

The detective, however, said he wouldn't be surprised if the investigation led to another suspect. They had a couple of them. Her husband gambled and had relations with dangerous casino people, one of whom was Isaac Moyo, a convicted murderer. He could be the mastermind.

And another thing, the detective continued, he still had his reservations about Agnes. 'Bad as she is,' he said, 'to kill, one had to have a strong motive,' and as things stood, they still hadn't established a strong enough motive. The phone records showed that behind Nolwazi's back, Thembani was going strong with Agnes. And sorry as he is to say it, phone records show that Thembani wanted to divorce her for Agnes. So if Agnes had killed Nolwazi, they would have understood, not the other way around.

There was silence for some days afterwards. And during those quiet few days, Detective Molapo only called her once to tell her the investigations were going well. The man who killed the man who killed her husband was Mozambican. He had fled to Mozambique, and they were on their way to get him.

Nolwazi's brother who lived in Vereeniging came and stayed a day, asking her not to do anything stupid. Such things happen, Sis, he said. She could tell he thought she was planning suicide. Her mother had thought the same. She did not understand how it happened that the two people who should know her better than anyone in the world knew so little about her.

It was on a Sunday morning that she awoke to the noise of her phone ringing. Groggily, she picked it up. It was Detective Molapo. He said he sought to see her at the police station first thing on Monday morning. Why? She would know when she arrived, he said. How was their journey to Mozambique, she asked, but he had dropped the call.

Driving along the flagstone paving on her way to the police station the following morning, she thought wryly that the old Ford with its screeching gears, was a burden, an announcement of how things had changed and nothing would ever be the same again. Her new Honda had been repossessed and auctioned off because money was still owed on it when Thembani died.

It renewed the pain in her heart to think that Thembani had let himself be fooled by that skank. How could someone abandon such peace as they had achieved? In her mind, their lives epitomised stability. She had never harassed him and he was always cautious never to harass her. They both knew the importance of apology and humility, and this had made their lives easy. She had imagined the two of them growing old together, becoming like one of those couples who spoke of a union half a century old.

The police station was next to a library, with a community centre on the right, and at the back, Balambile Mall. She parked near the gate of the library and contemplated her situation, wondering why she had been summoned. Could they have found out? How? No. They could not have done. They were only suspicious of her. It was their job. And yet, as her brother had said, *she*, not Agnes, must be the primary suspect: a scorned wife killing her husband who'd taken a lover was the theory, not an uncommon one. What they wanted was to question her, see if they could get something out of her. She felt weak with guilt. But then again, as always when her moral nature was failing, she contemplated the rectitude of what she had done. It always passed the test. She had been protecting herself, a victim, the one wronged. If she had not done what she did, she would have had to kill herself because she could not live with such betrayal. Nothing in her experience of life had prepared her for it.

It was the Mercedes ML that pushed her to bug his cellphone. He bought an ML with her, then suddenly, it was in Agnes' possession, and when she complained, he advised her to stop looking at Agnes as some devil but as the innocent mother of his child. At that time, he hardly spent a minute with her and he had developed a bad temper.

The cellphone bugging, however, brought very distasteful results. A conspiracy was hatched while she listened in. 'If we make another kid,' Thembani said to Agnes, 'she' – Nolwazi – 'will realize that she has no place in my life, and seek a divorce.' Asking for a divorce outright, Thembani said, when Agnes pushed him to be candid, would be callous, considering how far they had come. Nolwazi had listened to this and more. And knew she had to act swiftly.

Thembani and Agnes had planned for the bash a week earlier, and had agreed they would try for a baby that night, so she had had enough time to decide on the best way to put an end to the farce.

Finding Edmund wasn't hard. With the media proclaiming it every day, she knew that taxi drivers were the people to go to. The first one she approached, Maphosa, was the one to direct her to Edmund. He agreed but for so low a fee, she thought he was setting her up. It was also Maphosa who advised her about what he termed 'witness elimination', and connected her with the Peugeot man, saying it was what they specialized in.

'Wouldn't too many people then be involved?' Nolwazi had asked him, feeling that the involvement of the Peugeot man had weakened the secret.

'When Edmund gets caught, he'll blab,' Maphosa said. 'These men never get caught.'

'Why not get them to do the job straight?'

'They don't do big people because there are high risks of getting caught. These *yaope* guys do it because they don't mind getting caught.'

And the deal was done.

Edmund would do the job, the Peugeot guys would have him done in, and then they'd leave for Mozambique.

As she drew into the police parking lot, she was sure she had been a hundred per cent morally right.

The Way of Revenge

Valerie Tagwira

It was going to be his big night. Farai was confident that everything would go according to plan. His plan.

A week's preparation had been rather superfluous. But then, that was Fadzai's way. She was the bossy one. One had to understand his twin sister. After all she'd been diagnosed as being obsessive compulsive. How could his 'schizophrenic with arsonist tendencies' compete with that? His feeble attempt at humour had him grinning mirthlessly.

Give the bitch a fright, and then we can escalate gradually... chase her and her bastard out of town... even run her out of the country... Fadzai had said in an oddly calm tone.

She'd suggested that the initial episode could be staged around a mugging. 'A mugging!?' Farai recalled disdainfully. What an insult! Why waste his mathematician's brain planning a mugging? She might as well have hired a low-life Mbare thug for $5! He scowled, determined to do this his own way. That's why he had brought the two-litre container. Good thing Fadzai was oblivious to this little modification of her so-called plan.

Adrenaline coursed through his system and he felt a jolt of excitement. It had been such a long time since he last did something like this. To execute what he had in mind, someone with his disposition and his diagnosis was better suited to the task than Fadzai. His diagnosis enabled him to live out his most extreme fantasies and get away with them most of the time. Well, his younger self had. His biggest regret yet was getting fired from his university job. He would deal with the dean later. All in good time.

It was a typical, bitingly cold, June night. He felt a rare flicker of compassion for the countless beggars who slept on the streets of Harare, exposed to the unforgiving elements. As if in conspiracy with him, the night was as dark as he needed it to be. The lone tower light in the distance did little to improve general visibility. That, however, was inconsequential. Farai now knew the area just as well as he knew his target's routine.

For the second time that night, he strolled casually down Goto Street, blending seamlessly into the gloom. His black trousers and hoodie, a last minute brainwave, were a perfect camouflage. He hunched his shoulders forwards and adopted a posture intended to appear sinister and worthy of respect, the kind of respect which meant that anyone he met would steer clear of him. And people did keep their distance. This was Mbare. For all anybody knew, he could have been a hardened gangster. But then again, why not just another frustrated young man on his way home after the umpteenth unsuccessful day of job-hunting in the city? He smiled to himself.

It was only 7.30 p.m. but the usual Mbare street bustle was fast receding as more and more people retreated indoors to escape both the night and the cold. It didn't look as if there would be any potential witnesses. This suited him just fine. At the top of Goto Street, he hesitated ever so slightly before turning left and slinking into the sanitary lane adjacent to the back of the shack. His target's dwelling.

On a previous inspection of the surroundings, he'd already confirmed that there were no dogs in that neighbourhood. Luck was on his side. He couldn't take the risk of barking dogs raising attention to his presence, or worse still, attacking him.

The shack was right at the corner, and somewhat set apart from the main house and the other two shacks in the yard. Yet one more thing in his favour. Yes, the thrill of anticipating a spectacular outcome was overwhelming, but the situation had to be contained, at least to some extent. Only his intended target was supposed to get what was coming to her.

A surreptitious stroll down the sanitary lane confirmed it to be deserted. Gleefully thanking his ancestors for a dark, wintry June night, he walked back up to the shack. He could hear the muted sounds of music playing inside. It suggested that the woman was still awake, but it would also mask any noise that he might inadvertently make.

With efficient, practised movements he decanted the container quietly, soaking clear liquid into the wooden panels at the back of the small wooden dwelling. He inhaled the fumes, his excitement mounting. It was time for the closing act. At each corner of the back wall, he placed a full box of matches, making sure there was good contact with liquid dripping off the wall. He lit two cigarette stubs and attached one to each box. Quickly, he picked up the now empty container and walked briskly towards Mbare Market.

He would position himself near the northern entrance. From that vantage point, he would enjoy a clear view of the imminent inferno. He had just a few minutes to get there. Another surge of adrenaline propelled his feet forwards.

***

For the fifth time that evening, Fadzai washed her hands. She felt uneasy when she realised what she was doing, and what it meant. Her dose of Clomipramine had been reduced so as to alleviate the side effects that she'd been experiencing. For a while, she'd achieved good symptom control on the lower dose, but in the past few weeks, she'd found that the hair-brushing and the hand-washing in particular were again out of control.

Anxiety about her marriage was almost driving her insane. She spent long hours agonising about Tawana's affair, obsessing about whether or not he would leave her. She would question him relentlessly, only stopping when it appeared that he might lose his temper. She loved him, and she would do anything necessary to keep him.

On most days, Fadzai found herself having recurrent malicious thoughts about that wretched woman and her equally wretched baby. Six months had elapsed since discovery, but time had not healed her. It had strengthened her resolve to fight back.

She knew she could deal with the woman. The baby was the sticking point, and the more she thought about him, the more unsettled she became. Tawana had given his assurance that he would have nothing to do with them, but Fadzai was not so sure. What chance did she have against that baby when she had failed to conceive in five solid years?

She sighed, still determined that she would do whatever was necessary to preserve the integrity of her marriage. She ran a brush aggressively through her hair, then immediately stopped. She was doing it again. She would have to see her psychiatrist sooner than previously scheduled.

A quick glance at her watch told her that she barely had thirty minutes to get ready. Her husband was working late but he'd soon be home. Their dinner reservation at Meikles Hotel was for 8.30 p.m. As she showered, her mind drifted back to her conversation with her friend Julie earlier that week. It had been her second time to open up to anyone about her husband's infidelity with their domestic worker, the pregnancy, and the baby. The anger, hurt and humiliation still lingered, but she loved her husband, and she knew that he still loved her.

Julie had been clearly shocked. 'What? Are you seriously telling me that he had a baby with the domestic worker? Right under your nose?'

'Yes,' she had replied calmly.

'The bastard! Tell me you're getting a divorce,' her friend had immediately pressed.

'No such thing, my friend. I'm staying right here. I love him. Besides, I can't let that woman win,' she'd said simply.

'But how can you even bear to look at him? You must be crazy!' Julie had been disbelieving.

'Possibly,' Fadzai had responded, shrugging, but she had felt her temper rising at being so harshly criticised. Julie didn't have a right to be this judgemental.

'Look, this happened several months ago. I knew you would react like this. That's why I didn't tell you before. But I'm telling you now that I've dealt with it.'

Julie had continued shaking her head as Fadzai ploughed on in her husband's defence, 'He apologised. We fired the girl. The affair meant nothing. It was just a moment of weakness. He was extremely stressed. We both were. We'd been having problems. All that stress of trying to get pregnant... all that fuss with travelling to South Africa for tests and

IVF, the expense, the miscarriage...'

Julie interrupted. 'I hear you Fadzai. But can you stop and listen to yourself? Why is it all about *him*? What about you? Were you not stressed as well? Did you run off and have an affair? He should have been more protective, more supportive... not cheat on you! And this girl now has *his* baby! Are you so naive as to think that it's over just like that?' Her voice had risen. She'd been plainly disappointed.

Fadzai had been equally mutinous. 'Let's leave it, shall we?' She'd snapped. What right did Julie have to judge her? Or to offer her any kind of advice? She who'd never been married. She who had a string of failed relationships! The rest of their conversation had been stilted and Julie had left in a huff. They had not spoken since.

Despite her concerns, Fadzai was sure that the whole nightmare would recede into the past. The plan was in motion to hound the woman and her baby out of their lives. She trusted Farai to help her. As twins they'd always looked out for each other. Besides, he owed her. Ever since he'd been fired from his lecturer job, she'd been looking after him.

She was startled out of her reverie by a text message alert beep on her phone.

'Done!' was the short and precise message from her brother.

She felt a wave of triumph. Uplifted, she finished getting ready. It was almost time. She slipped into her favourite black shift and appraised herself in the mirror. She looked good. A light touch of foundation and a dusting of powder transformed her skin to the flawless shade of her youth. Smiling, she styled her hair in an upswept hairdo. She wanted to look good for her husband on this special night. He might not know it yet, but they had the sweetness of revenge to celebrate.

Realising that they would definitely not make it in time for their booking, she picked up her phone and speed-dialled Tawana. She tapped her foot and listened while it rang out.

She waited about fifteen minutes, then speed-dialled again. She spoke as soon as she heard the answering click.

'Hey, Tawana darling, we're really late for our reservation. Can we meet at Meikles instead of you picking me up from home?'

There was a momentary silence at the other end, and then a woman spoke. 'Hullo Ma'am. I'm answering this phone for a certain gentleman.

He can't talk to you right now. Who are you, if I may ask?'

A woman answering her husband's phone? And how dare she question her? Fadzai was upset and was immediately on the offensive. 'Well, who are you? I'm his wife and I demand that you hand him his phone immediately.'

There was an audible intake of breath, before the woman continued. 'My name is Detective Sango; I need you to confirm if your husband is Tawana Dombo, who drives a black BMW X6 Sedan.'

A police officer? Fadzai's anger instantly gave way to alarm and confusion.

'Yes, that's my husband's name and he does drive such a car,' she replied cautiously.

'I'm afraid there has been a terrible accident Ma'am. I need you to go to Harare Hospital Police Post as soon as possible. I will meet you there...'

Fadzai interrupted, 'What... an accident? Is my husband okay? What happened? Where is he?'

'Ma'am, please, let's meet at Harare Hospital Police Post,' the officer repeated.

An entanglement of confused questions competed for articulation, clogging up Fadzai's throat. She managed a croaky, 'Please...could you at least tell me what has happened to my husband?' She was close to tears.

'Ma'am, it's really better if you go to Harare Hospital...'

Fadzai pleaded, 'Please, I need to know now, *please* tell me what has happened.'

The police officer sighed, then explained, 'Okay, Ma'am, we're investigating and we still have more witnesses to interview. What we do know is that there was a fire in Mbare. It appears your husband was driving past and he stopped to help. He bravely saved a woman and her baby from the fire, but Ma'am, I'm afraid he was badly burnt. He didn't....'

Fadzai interrupted, incredulous. 'My husband? He's at work in town, not in Mbare. No, no, what you're saying is impossible...' It just didn't make sense. She could have understood Tawana being liable for a road traffic accident. He had a weakness for speeding and reckless driving. But a fire in Mbare? Why had he been there in the first place?

Then a possibility dawned over her. It must have something to do with that woman. But he had promised…Then another realisation… Farai and his morbid fascination for starting fires. But that had been in the past, and he had been taking his medication! What had *he* done? What had *they* done? She felt her head spinning, and she was swaying, losing balance.

'Ma'am are you still there? I'm so sorry, your husband didn't make it. I have his ID but I need you to come over and assist us with identifying his body at the hospital.'

Fadzai's mobile phone slipped from her hand and crashed to the floor. Slowly she bent down to pick it up, her heart filled with grief, her mind with fear. How would she live with the knowledge of what she had done?

Now, she would never be able to talk to anyone not about her brother's illness or obsession, her husband's affair, nor the woman in Mbare nor her baby.

… And what if they claimed a part of his estate?

Heaven's Embassy

Chris Wilson

Mrs Chipunza had done well, realising there is money in property development and pushing her husband Bernard into that line of business. He now built houses for people, mostly in the Diaspora sending money home. Plus, of course, those who had suddenly made a lot out of diamonds, or simply by being in the government. They had two sons at a private school in Mutare, not far from their home in Murambi Drive, right opposite the golf course.

Mrs Chipunza was also an active member of Heaven's Embassy, in fact she was their 'ambassador' in Mutare.

'The chosen representative of Jesus himself!' Bernard used to boast.

They had given her a laptop and 48-inch flat screen with tall speakers and a USB port, and every week sent her the latest sermons and hymns to download and play to the congregation which gathered at her house on Sunday mornings and Wednesday evenings. They would come, mostly women for some reason, in their very best, complete with hats or headdresses, high heels and handbags, to praise the Lord, sing and clap hands, stomp their feet and waggle their bottoms. And, of course, leave a small monetary donation to ensure their visa to Heaven.

Mrs Chapunza had used part of the loot to extend the garage and turn it into a real church, with a coloured glass window and the TV on the altar. When it was not being used for God's purposes, their two sons were in there playing video games. They had a computer in their bedroom of course, but preferred the large screen.

Recently the 'Embassy' had also paid for Mrs Chipunza to fly to Nigeria for a three-day celebration with delegates from all over the world. She met Pastor Sam Obiekwe himself, realised as soon as she saw him that none of the stories about him could possibly be true. What a pack of vicious lies! He was just so handsome and charming, quite clearly filled with divine light, and she came back with a dozen stunning Nigerian outfits with which to completely outshine anything any member of her congregation back home dared wear.

Mai Jane was a quiet woman. She was like a mouse, people didn't really notice her but she never missed a meeting and sang fervently and devoutly. She was a widow, with a son, Genius, who, despite his name and having done so well at school, was working as someone's gardener in South Africa. She lived in Dangamvura, a suburb right out of town, almost a separate one in itself, a poor place with even more sporadic electricity than the rest of the country and, for years now, no running water at all. A limited amount was delivered each week in a dirty bowser.

When her husband was alive they had begun building a small brick house there. The cement slab had been laid, and the walls were a foot high when he died. He had worked for a white man, a Mr Partridge, who had paid for his funeral and given her enough money to finish the house, but which they found necessary to use instead to survive while Genius hunted unsuccessfully for work. Eventually he, like so many others, found himself in South Africa, by which time Mr Partridge's business had closed down and he had left for Australia.

So the house had remained like that for the past five years. Mai Jane had had to leave the place she rented and move into the iron shed that they had initially put up when they were allocated their stand. She tried to do a bit of cross-border trading, so many other ladies were doing it, even doing well out of it. But for some reason she did not. She found she had no head for money, she got muddled, she was cheated, she was not hard-nosed enough. All that wheeler-dealing, that bartering and bargaining, haggling for every precious cent exhausted her. And the border crossings were a nightmare. Any profit she might have made was extorted out of her.

She retreated, and lived alone, Genius sent what little money he could. She tried growing rape, covo and tomatoes to sell but the Dangamvura soil was poor and the water situation went from bad to worse. However, once a week, she would put on a smart pink dress and take the crowded mini-bus to town, then begin the long walk up to Murambi Drive.

She had joined the 'Embassy' in better days, when they had had a bit of money, and she could appear as well-heeled as the rest of the congregation. And still, although there were plenty of other churches much closer to where she lived, she remained loyal to it. Or perhaps it was rather to Jesus himself. The feeling that ignited in her when they sang was addictive. Jesus would not let her down. She did not appear to notice they all looked down on her, on her shabby shoes, her poverty and dare one say it? Her very black skin!

One day she received a notice from the town council saying that she was hindering the "development of the area" and if her house was not completed within six months the stand would be reallocated. She didn't know what to do, who to turn to, and had to wait a whole day till the electricity came back and she could go to a neighbour to charge her phone. Finally, she managed to send a note to Genius.

His first thought was to turn to his employer. He was a sympathetic person and Genius wondered how to broach the subject with him? But what could he reasonably be expected to do? It was not his problem; it was nobody's but their own. His and his mother's.

Genius and Mark Partridge, son of his late father's employer, had been, for a while, at Mutare Boys' High together. They had both been keen gymnasts. Mark had his own set of parallel bars and a trampoline at home and they used to practice for hours, competing with each other to do ever more daring feats. Mark had muscular arms, he excelled on the high bar, but he could not beat Genius when it came to somersaults and back flips. Genius could do twenty flick flacks in a row, backwards or forwards. They both had wild dreams of representing Zimbabwe at the Olympics. Once the Zim Zim Acrobats came to town for a show, inspiring ideas of joining a circus! Or failing that, a glamorous life of crime. With their agility they could easily scale walls and leap from rooftop to rooftop: they would make excellent burglars.

And yet now look at them, Mark an accountant or something in Australia, while he, Genius, of all people, was mowing somebody's lawn!

It was a shot in the dark but Genius wrote to him via Facebook. And sometimes amazing things happen. Mark told his father and, to Genius's utter incredulity, Mr Partridge offered to send $10,000. 'Don't tell my wife' he wrote. 'This is between you and me. But your father was a good man and my heart is still in Zimbabwe. It always will be.'

The money arrived via Western Union. Genius did not have a bank account so just kept it in a tin in his room. He was not too concerned, the property was secure with an electric fence and alarms everywhere. And he always kept his door locked.

He texted his mother to say he would be sending an initial sum, she was to order bricks, cement, pit and river sand. 'At least try to get the walls up and then we can work on the roof. If they see we are actually doing something they should give us an extension.'

Mai Jane was overcome. 'Thank you Jesus,' she kept saying, over and over again. 'Thank you, thank you.'

Next day after church she asked Mrs Chipunza if she could have a word. Mrs Chipunza, surprised that Mai Jane had any money at all, said she would speak to her husband, was sure he would be able to help.

Next day she texted. 5,000 bricks, twenty-five bags of cement, two loads of pit sand and ten wheelbarrows of river sand would come to $1000. As she was a member of the congregation her husband would not charge for delivery and would even supply a bricklayer at no extra cost. Mai Jane texted Genius, he sent up the money with Western Union and she took it straight to Mrs Chipunza, terrified she might lose it or get robbed on the way.

Weeks passed, nothing happened.

Nothing was ever delivered.

Every week after church Mrs Chipunza would come rushing over: 'I know, I know, I know! I'm as frustrated as you! So is Bernard, he has been on the phone to those people the whole week. They just come up with one excuse after the other. But don't worry, it will all be sorted out soon. Just have faith and trust in the Lord. Oh and Jane, don't mention this to any of the others here, you know how people are.'

Genius was doubly frustrated being so far away. 'Ask her for the money back and get someone else,' he texted a dozen times. Not especially religious himself, Genius nevertheless believed the church had a role in society, and if it gave the poor hope what was wrong with that? Of course there were the charlatans, the so-called prophets, the shameless scams. The sex scandal involving Pastor Sam, and his claim to be able to cure HIV had been big news. But, up to now, Genius had kept his thoughts to himself, happy that it provided his mother with some spiritual release from her hard life.

Now he began thinking otherwise.

He just could not understand Mrs Chapunza's behaviour. If this was a plot for a movie or a story it would seem implausible. Why would she do this? Take money and not deliver the goods, knowing that if the story got out her reputation and lucrative position as Jesus's ambassador would be ruined? It was not even that big a sum, especially for someone like her. It was not logical, did not make sense. But then why did Pastor Sam himself impregnate all those women knowing his reputation would be on the line? Why claim to be able to cure HIV or speak in tongues when it can clearly be proven otherwise? Why indeed! Why do our President, his wife, the entire government, the police, the army, three quarters of the population, do the things they do without the slightest hint of shame or embarrassment?

He kept insisting his mother confront Mrs Chipunza, but it was always difficult for Mai Jane to catch her alone. She did not want to say anything in front of anyone else, and after church there were always so many ladies gathering round and laughing and admiring each other's outfits and complimenting Mrs Chipunza on hers. But eventually, one Sunday, she lingered in the background until at last they were alone. She stepped out of the shadows and gave a little curtsy. 'Forgive me Ma'am, but my son says I am to ask for the money back and find someone else.'

Mrs Chipunza looked at her, took a deep breath. 'My dear! I know you have been very patient. And God will reward you for that. I will speak to Bernard.'

'If I could just have the money back...'

'Oh my dear, there's no need for that. It's just a matter of chasing up those suppliers. Bernard phones them every day and assures me that he, personally, is taking care of the matter. Why back out now when we are so close to getting it done? Far better to deal with people you know and can trust. This construction business is notorious, practically every person you meet is a shark.'

'But time is running out, the council are going to reallocate.'

'I know, I know. Leave it to me,' said Mrs Chipunza.

Another week passed. That Sunday Mai Jane was there before anyone else. She had an idea. 'Ma'am, what if we tell the whole congregation and ask them all to pray to get the job done?'

'Oh, I wouldn't do that' said Mrs Chipunza. 'Not yet. We don't want to bother God with problems we can easily solve ourselves. God helps those who help themselves, you know that! But listen, I have a proposal. I've spoken to Bernard and he agrees. You need to complete not only your walls, but the entire house as soon as possible. It is going to require more money of course. But there is no point starting if you can't finish.'

Mai Jane assured her. 'As I told you my son has another nine thousand dollars ready.'

'Yes but that was three months ago. Does he still have it? You know how things are these days. It is hard to hang on to savings. You should invest it all at once before he fritters it away.'

'I know,' said Mai Jane, suddenly worried. Perhaps she was right, how did she know that Genius still had the money?

'What we will do is this. You are going to need door frames, window frames, corrugated iron, even more bricks and cement, bathroom fittings. Bernard estimates another $5000 will cover it. Of course, he will get the best deals for you but he will need the cash in hand, the full amount. As soon as you can get it he is going to pull out all the stops to get your house completed on time.'

Mai Jane filled with misgiving. She waited till she got all the way home before texting Genius, knowing he would be angry and terrified at the same time that he would say he had been forced to use the money for something else. But what she was even more afraid of was that he would refuse to send it, and how would she explain that to Mrs Chipunza?

Genius could not believe it. Here was his mother wanting to give that woman more money, when she had not even supplied the first order! How could she be so stupid? But his impatience with his timid, humble mother gave way to growing anger at the thought of her in the hands of that crook, that bitch, that bloody woman!

It was a Sunday and supposed to be his day off but his employer had asked him to help clear out the storeroom which was full of junk that needed to be thrown away. Including a monkey suit that somebody had once worn to a fancy dress party. Old and shabby, made of brown velvety stuff with a long tail and cartoonish face, holes where the eyes should be, it was more or less his size. It gave him an idea. He wondered if he could still leap and somersault as he used to? Gardening kept him pretty fit, but… He tried a couple of back flips on the grass. Yes, he was still in good shape.

He asked his employer for a week's leave, explained that his mother needed some help and arranged for a friend, another Zimbabwean, to come over to cut the grass while he was gone.

By coincidence the maximum amount Western Union would send in one go was exactly $5,000. The remaining four seemed to dwindle in the tin back in his room. He handed the cash over, gave them his mother's name. The woman gave him the print out and highlighted the MTC number for him to send, but he kept that for later.

He set off early next morning; the bus was at Beitbridge by midday and the passengers joined the long hot queue at immigration. The whole process took five tortuous hours, they were insulted and pushed around as always, sour thoughts on every traveller's face. But Genius had done it before, knew the ropes, and kept his temper. He spent the night in Gloria's Guest House and next day took a ZUPCO bus to Masvingo, then another to Mutare.

Another day, two breakdowns and seventeen police checkpoints later, he arrived, covered in dust, smelling of sweat. He checked into another guest house under a false name. Ate, slept, avoided talking to anyone, charged his phone.

Next morning he called his mum. 'The money is there. You MUST collect it this morning. Get Mrs Chipunza to meet you at Western Union and give it straight to her. Don't walk in the street with it, make sure she comes with you and give it to her right there in the shop.'

He texted her the MTC number.

***

By midday the news was all over town. Mrs Chapunza had been robbed. She had been downtown on some errand, arrived back home, used her remote to open the gate and driven in. As she got out of the car a figure – she swore it was a large monkey, or a baboon – leapt down off the roof and snatched her car keys. She gave a short cry and dropped everything. The air stuck in her throat. She stood stock still, hands in the air. The ape gibbered at her, bouncing up and down, jingling the keys. Then he dropped them, grabbed her Gucci bag off the ground, stroked the expensive leather appreciatively, smelled it, tasted it, stuck his face right inside it, then ran whooping down the driveway, vaulted over the gate and was gone.

Everyone was talking, texting, phoning, visiting, eager for details, forming theories. Of course it was not a real monkey but the image of a large ape stuck and grew, became almost superhuman. Which somehow made it more believable. A mere mortal would not dare challenge Mrs Chapunza.

The news however did not make it out to Mai Jane in Dangamvura.

That Sunday at church all the ladies oozed with sympathy. 'It must have been terrifying,' said Mrs Chidzikwe. 'You are so brave,' said Mrs Morangazvombo.

Mrs Chapunza wore a tragic look. She had indeed suffered. 'But I knew God was with me' she said. 'And the police found my bag! My lovely Gucci bag! Without the money of course.' The ladies were too polite to enquire exactly how much, they assumed it was not such a great amount, nobody would be stupid enough to carry more cash than absolutely necessary. No, it was not the money, it was the trauma, the shock, the humiliation she must have suffered. Poor Mrs Chapunza.

Mai Jane, who had arrived late and only just cottoned on to what they were talking about, began to look agitated. Mrs Chapunza caught her eye, and made a very slight movement with her hand that no one else noticed but which effectively silenced her. Then she raised her hands and eyes towards Heaven. 'Hallelujah!' She began singing and everyone else joined in louder than ever.

A million miles above the sky
Angels bow before your throne
You are God and God alone

Afterwards she took Mai Jane aside. 'I need a word with you my dear, as soon as everyone has gone.'

So Mai Jane knew.

As the last lady waved goodbye Mrs Chapunza led her onto her veranda and made her sit down. "My dear, I have bad news, I wanted to tell you in person, not on the phone. The money that was stolen was yours. But don't start worrying. The police are on the case. Bernard has made sure of that. And the Lord is watching over us, let us just keep calm and wait.'

'But what if they don't get it back?'

'Just have faith. Everything will work out for the best. But as I said before, don't mention it to anyone.'

Mai Jane walked like a zombie back down the hill. What was she going to say to Genius? *Just have faith, just have faith…* she repeated the words over and over. And prayed to Lord Jesus to please help the police find her money. Even though she knew from first-hand experience that faith in God was one thing, faith in the police quite another.

Back home she simply sat on the front step of her unfinished house and stared as it grew slowly dark.

Safely back in South Africa Genius was waiting.

He was scared but exhilarated. The whole thing had worked out so easily and he did not feel sorry or guilty at all. It was his own money, he reasoned, that he had stolen back. Well 99 per cent of it anyway. There had been a bit extra which he had had to take to make it seem a real robbery. He was glad her phone had not been in the bag so he had not been obliged to take that as well. There had not even been a bank card or a driving license. Perhaps people like her did not need such things?

He felt no remorse. He had not hurt her. He retained the vision of her trapped by the open car door, her stuff scattered on the ground. Even then, when he was threatening her with his antics, and her cap of artificial hair was awry, she had seemed inviolable, small eyes, sour mouth, fleshy neck, nothing bad could ever happen to her.

He was only sorry for his own mother, that he was putting her through more suffering. But, if things worked out as he hoped they would… He decided it was time to send her a short story he had written himself. He was rather proud of it, it sounded like it really had come from the Bible.

***

Another week passed.

Mai Jane arrived at church early, on tenterhooks. Any news? Mrs Chapunza sighed. 'No my dear, just be patient. The Lord works in mysterious ways.'

The other ladies arrived, concern for Mrs Chapunza had reached new heights as the story had been spread and embroidered. The image of the leaping figure had grown. It had swung down from a tree, blotting out the sky and bared its terrible fangs. Even then she had been so brave, had not flinched, had not screamed. 'God was watching over you,' they all agreed.

Mai Jane listened, her thoughts confused, her emotions running high. She was close to breaking down in front of everyone, throwing herself onto the floor and imploring Lord Jesus to notice, to do something, for them all to notice, to do something! Just for once!

But Mrs Chapunza, while leading the service and smiling and accepting their compliments, kept her in check with a firm eye.

She tried to have a word afterwards but Mrs Chapunza was off somewhere in a hurry. 'Another week' she said. Mai Jane felt exhausted, too feeble to protest. She felt she would faint. For the first time Mrs Chapunza's voice lost its sweetness, became hard. 'Pull yourself together, Mai. Count your blessings! Remember Philippians Chapter 4, Verse six. *Do not fret or have anxiety about anything, just let your requests be known unto God.'*

Mai Jane stumbled off down the road. A car stopped. 'Are you all right? Can I give you a lift?'

It was Mrs Mhlanga. She insisted she get in. They drove down towards the bus terminus. And it was on the way that Mai Jane did what she had tried so hard not to do, she could not stop herself and the whole story came pouring out along with her tears. Mrs Mhlanga drove her all the way to Dangamvura and for the first time saw the pitiful way she lived. Mai Jane got out of the car, fumbled with her phone and silently handed it to Mrs Mhlanga to read the little story her son had sent.

'Can you forward that to me?' asked Mrs Mhlanga.

In no time everyone knew. And if Mai Jane had been able to eavesdrop on every conversation, she would have kicked herself for not having said something sooner.

Mrs Mhlanga phoned Mrs Chidzikwe who came straight over. 'Of course, she must pay back the money,' they agreed. 'No, it was not her fault, it was stolen but that is no excuse. She was responsible for it. If she was poor herself it would be a different matter but she is not. And for her to have let the whole matter slide by, hoping no one would mention it, is an insult to all!'

Mrs Chidzikwe phoned Mrs Morangazvombo. Mrs Morangazvombo went straight over to Mrs Nandoro's house. Mrs Manyika was already there. Things had begun to crack. Something dormant slowly woke. The ground rumbled and briefly opened revealing red rivers of blood. Long repressed resentments rose to the surface and boiled over. Jealousies. Grudges. Everyone had a story to tell, steam to let off. The way she preens herself in front of everyone, expects us to admire her outfits, boasts about her silly children with their smart phones. My son got better marks than hers at school but do I have to gloat about it? No! All those airs and graces. And that monstrosity of a house! Have you heard the way she talks to men? That sugary voice she puts on? Poor Bernard. She once made a pass at my husband! And mine! Do you know she beats her housemaid? And goes months without bothering to pay her? How much of our money has she stolen? Our humble offerings?

But who was going to confront her?

***

That Sunday Mai Jane was not at church.

Mrs Chapunza was in a purple and white outfit, with a matching headdress. 'Let us pray,' she said and they all knelt and closed their eyes.

But somehow today things were not so fervent. And the singing was muted.

It was Mrs Mhlanga's turn to read from the Bible. She stood up and held it in her hands, but read from her phone, which was inside it, instead:

Once a poor man gave his neighbour, who was equally poor, his only thing of value, a gold ring, for safekeeping. Shortly after the neighbour came to him in great distress, saying he had been robbed, the ring had been stolen and he did not know what to do, he felt responsible and yet there was no way he could replace it. Both men cried, their families cried too, but all agreed there was nothing to be done and the most important thing was that they remained good friends and neighbours and help each other as much as they can.

The ladies all murmured their approval.

Another time a poor man gave a rich neighbour his only thing of value, a gold ring, for safekeeping. The wealthy man was robbed, and the ring was stolen. The wealthy man, remembering Jesus's words, immediately came to him and explained what had happened and insisted on giving him its full value, which he accepted, since the man was rich and could afford it. And they continued living next door to each other happily.

They all concurred this was the best outcome possible.

And once, there was a poor woman who went to a rich woman and gave her her life savings, advance payment for a small house.

Mrs Chapunza had had her eyes devoutly closed. Now she opened them wide.

The rich woman was robbed, the money was stolen and she simply said there was nothing she could do about it. It was not her fault so she felt no obligation towards the poor woman at all. She was sorry about it of course, but it was just a case of bad luck.

Mrs Mhlanga closed the Bible over her phone. 'Now, I would like to ask the gathering here today, what do you think she should have done?'

Silence.

Mrs Chapunza's eyes narrowed.

Who would be first?

The ladies all looked at each other. Mrs Morangazvombo took a deep breath. Mrs Nandoro looked scared. It was Mrs Mhlanga herself who began, but one by one they all came forward, hesitant, in need of prompting, but eventually each had her say. They were unanimous. The rich woman had behaved wrongly. Jesus would not have approved and there was absolutely no way she was going to get into Heaven now. Unless...

Suddenly Mrs Chidzikwe fell onto her knees. Her eyes rolled back in her head and her mouth fell open. 'That woman is among us! At this very moment! I feel her presence!' She raised her hands, looked up at the ceiling. 'Let her step forward and confess. Let her be purged of her sin! Oh Lord, let her identify herself.'

Mrs Chapunza remained silent, skeptical, sneering even. Such theatrics were her specialty, Mrs Chidzikwe's attempts were amateur, ludicrous. But it seemed she did have a mutiny on her hands. One by one the ladies all began clamouring, clapping and chanting, 'Let her step forward and identify herself.'

Mrs Chapunza rose. Her breasts heaved. She looked quite magnificent. Her smooth shoulders rose out of the ruffles round the wide neck of her dress. She looked at them, their hysteria mounting and then her voice thundered out: 'Jesus lifted up himself, and said unto them, he that is without sin among you, let him cast the first stone!'

She stood there, commanding, daring them to rise against her. 'Mrs Chidzikwe! You say you feel her presence, call upon her to confess and yet you are unable to name her? I call upon you to do so!'

Mrs Chidzikwe rose up off the floor, her hair lopsided, opened her mouth then shut it again.

'Mrs Morangazvombo? Mrs Mhlanga?'

They all looked at each other nervously.

'This is a church!' proclaimed Mrs Chipunza. 'Not the house of a *n'anga!* The place for a witchhunt! How dare you insult our Lord with your primitive religion! We are modern people here. *Pamberi ne* Zimbabwe!' She glared round the room. 'And if you really want to name names we all know who voted for who in the last election!'

The ladies shuffled uncomfortably. Mrs Chipunza waited. At last she lowered her voice. 'Come. Let us end by doing what we came here to do. Let us sing to the Lord.' She pressed the remote, the TV flickered on, there was the calming sound of the piano and then the face and stirring voice of Frank Ugochukwu Edwards (AKA Richboy):

I see him
Standing by the door
With fire in his eyes
And healing in his wings
He's waiting for you

They gathered round the television and joined in.

***

A couple of days later Mai Jane was coming back from the bowser with a can of water. A truck had stopped beside her shed and three men were busy shovelling sand off the back. She gaped in disbelief. Later the same truck came by with bags of cement. The next day the bricks arrived and a bricklayer but there was no water to mix the cement. The bricklayer made a single call on his mobile and an hour later an overflowing bowser arrived, just for that purpose. Nothing, it seemed, was impossible.

Doors, windows, sheets of corrugated iron followed, wooden roof trusses, panes of glass. Bernard Chipunza himself came out to check on how things were going. In ten days the house was complete. Painted blue, with a red door.

Mrs Chipunza herself arrived, in full regalia, with a photographer from the Mutare Post. Mai Jane was speechless. Tears poured down.

'I don't know how to thank you.'

'My dear, thank the Lord not me.' Mrs Chipunza put on a saintly smile and posed like a celebrity for a photograph, handing Mai Jane the brand new set of keys.

Next day the picture was in the paper, an example of Heaven Embassy's wonderfully charitable work.

At church Mai Jane was shy but exultant. She had lots of photos on her phone to show the ladies. She could not stop laughing, pointing out every little feature. The washbasin, the shower fittings, even the toilet and the septic tank!

Mrs Chipunza smiled modestly. 'It was meant to be a surprise for poor Mai Jane' she explained. 'The reason for the delay was that we wanted to get everything together so that we could just get it all done in one go.'

The ladies fell over themselves to congratulate her and the singing that day was louder than ever.

Halle - lu

Halle – lu – lia

We lift our voices to praise your name

Printed in the United States
By Bookmasters